THE MILLION DOLLAR REAL ESTATE TEAM

How I Went from Zero to Earning $1 Million after Expenses in Three Years

by
Chris Watters
with
Bradley Pounds

The Million Dollar Real Estate Team: How I Went from
Zero to Earning $1 Million after Expenses in Three Years

Published in the United States.
WIR Publishing
ISBN-13: 978-0692905661
ISBN: 0692905669
Library of Congress Control Number: 2017909742

Design and illustrations by Leslie Kell
kellcreative.com

Edited by Kathryn Rogers
rogers-editorial.com

CONTENTS

PREFACE

(5)
Reasons You
Shouldn't Read This Book

I'm going to be honest with you; to say that this book is not for everyone is an understatement. For starters, the information contained in these pages is for real estate agents only, and only a small percentage of real estate agents at that. The agents who have what it takes to implement the accelerated growth strategies detailed in the following chapters are few and far between.

I wrote this book for agents who want to build businesses. Contrary to your big-box brokerage programming, if you are a single-agent operator, you are NOT building a business. You are not developing an asset that is saleable or one that would continue to provide for your family if you died tomorrow. Rather, you have a profitable but fragile practice that does not exist without you. Chances are that, if you are intellectually curious enough to read this book, your practice is one of the good ones. But a business, it is not — at least not yet.

In the following chapters, I'm going to tell you how I created in excess of $1 million in net income (after expenses) in just three years, using the team model. I've been told by industry leaders that I hit that benchmark faster than anyone else using this model. The success we've experienced is not a fluke; it's the result of a system and an organized approach to exponential growth.

That's not to say that it was smooth-sailing to get here. Hell, I've made so many costly mistakes that I've lost count. I wish this book had been around when I was getting started. I wrote it so that you could take what I learned along the way and, hopefully, skip most of the pitfalls.

But before you begin, you should know that saying this process is "challenging" or "difficult" does not even begin to capture the reality.

Following this path is going to kick your ass.

The life balance between work, friends, and spending time with your significant other — throw all that out the window. There is no such thing as work-life balance when you're building a team. Being present in the moment? Sometimes it's just not possible.

Most agents are lacking one or all of the following components necessary to make life easier when building a team: cash, previous experience in scaling business operations, sales volume, lead conversion chops, and leadership skills. Unless you have all of these things in spades, anticipate that there will be a HUGE learning curve as you transform your business.

 ## Here's what your learning curve will look like:

You will spin dozens of plates, and you will drop a few, and they will break.

You will become the go-to person for clients and staff alike — for everything.

You will have to make big decisions with no time to think them through.

You will hire the wrong people and suffer the consequences.

You will eventually be forced to fire someone you consider a friend.

At times, money will be tight. Your revenue is high but you have to reinvest most of it back into the business, so you should expect to live in a way that's more financially conservative than before.

If you think you've made a mistake by starting this journey, nobody would blame you for tapping out. It's better to know now, right?

Still curious? Let me persuade you further that this book is not for you.

THERE ARE *FIVE* VERY GOOD REASONS YOU SHOULD STOP WASTING TIME AND PUT DOWN THIS BOOK RIGHT NOW:

1. **You want to practice real estate for the rest of your life.** You can't think of ANYTHING you'd rather do than show property until 8:30 p.m., just to turn around the next day and prospect for sellers by knocking on doors in 90-degree heat. After giving listing presentations for years, you find them just as exhilarating as the very first time you sat down with an unreasonable seller. Growing as a leader, building a team of stellar folks around you and eventually firing yourself from day-to-day operations sounds like a lot of unnecessary effort and responsibility. Who wants that kind of pressure? You like life in the trenches and want to stay a practicing real estate agent forever. Owning a successful business that makes money whether or not you're in the office sounds like a pipe dream, and above all else, you are a realist.

2. **You don't want more control of your time.** Hey, remember the pitiful look your daughter gave you that time you were 30 minutes late for her soccer game . . . two weeks in a row? That was awesome. Oh, and how about the time you finally earned enough in commissions to feel OK about splurging on a family vacation to Hawaii . . . but you spent the whole trip glued to your phone, negotiating repairs and answering sign calls? Your significant other still won't let you live that one down, yeah? It's a good thing that your buyers and sellers know that they can call or text you at any hour of the night and you'll usually answer. So they do, and you love them for it! Thank goodness your overflowing calendar is there to tell you what to do, stacked full of everything but time for yourself. That's just fine by you, since you can't really remember who you were and what hobbies you enjoyed before you became an agent anyway!

3. **You're already an ace at all areas of business.** Since you're already a 10 out of 10 when it comes to customer service, lead generation, and appointment conversion — why bother getting better? Should you get a wild hair and decide

to build a team, it's a good thing that you're instinctively an amazing recruiter and know how to spot exactly the right talent. Because you've already mastered the technology arena by creating an easy to use, scalable database and back office process, you should definitely put your feet up. As a naturally gifted leader who, coincidentally, never ever misses the mark on expensive advertising campaigns, you've totally got this down.

4. **You're not willing to invest in yourself.** You work hard for your money and you're going to spend every penny of your well-earned commissions however you want, damn it! You go, girl/guy! Building a financial cushion to protect you from market changes is for nervous nellies who don't have faith in themselves to just make more money next quarter. Investing 90% of your returns back into the business seems foolish when you realize it would mean waiting another year or two to upgrade to the new Mercedes-Benz model. With 20-inch wheels and air-conditioned seats on the line, it's pretty clear that you have to buy it right now.

5. **You're not _____ enough.** This is the BIG one and my personal favorite because you can fill it in with anything you want! Can't think of anything? Here are some suggestions: You didn't finish college or pursue an MBA, so clearly you're not educated enough to run a business. And even before that, let's be honest; you weren't exactly the ambitious kid with the lemonade stand, so obviously you aren't cut out to be an entrepreneur. Come to think of it, you basically fell ass-backwards into a career as a respected, productive agent, didn't you? It's not like your efforts and work ethic created that success, so we can add 'not persistent enough' to the list. You don't totally understand how mortgage insurance works and sometimes can't remember which box to check on that obscure addendum, so there's all the proof we need that you're not smart enough. Take into consideration the fact that you began your real estate career while already in your 40s and, well, it goes without saying that you're not young enough, doesn't it?

And yet, you're still reading. I'm going to take that to mean that at least part of you wants MORE. Maybe you're thinking that you want your life back. You genuinely miss your spouse, your friends, and hobbies. Maybe you want to create college funds for your kids and better sleep for yourself because you know that their futures are secure.

At the same time, the real estate treadmill is killing you, taking its toll on your physical health and sanity each day. You need to know that there's a light at the end of the tunnel, that you will reap the rewards of your hard work. Perhaps you're still reading because you keep bumping your head on the same ceiling of what you're able to produce by yourself. You haven't disqualified yourself on the basis of not being good enough, but you're self-aware enough to realize that you don't know everything.

> *So know this:*
> *you're going to need help,*
> *and you're going to need a plan.*
>
>

INTRODUCTION

"Let's burn the whole thing down."

I heard myself say those words about my own business in December of 2011. For a second, one of my sales agents (and my co-author on this book), Bradley Pounds, looked at me as if deciding whether a psychiatric hold was in order.

"Why would you say that?" he finally asked. "We're doing great. We're making MONEY. It's the middle of the recession and I'm making MONEY." The panic was apparent.

Admittedly, it did sound crazy to even think about razing our brokerage to the ground and starting over. But I knew in my gut that there was a better way to grow our business as quickly and profitably as possible. I could see the next decade of slow, incremental growth and perpetual struggle unfolding before me, and I didn't like it.

Can you relate?

Have you ever wanted more control over your real estate business?

Ever feel like you can't jump off the real estate merry-go-round of listing appointments, showing properties, and handling one transactional crisis after another?

If you're reading this book, chances are that you're a real estate agent producing a healthy 30+ transaction sides per year and you've made something of a name for yourself as an individual broker/agent in your market. You've built that business (and reputation) by offering high-quality service to your clients. Those clients refer you their friends and family members, which in turn grows your business organically. You're a jack-of-all-trades but reasonably competent at all of the important elements that make for a good client experience—AND you're turning a profit. Your super-satisfied client

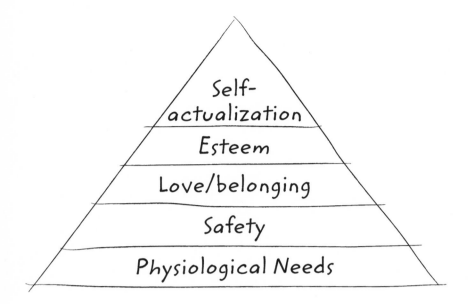

base is a source of pride for you, and your customers may even feel like extended family.

If we look back, we'll probably see that your early career was launched through brute force efforts, a few great decisions, and a bit of divine intervention. Unlike the 90% of new agents who struggle and fail out of the business, you raced up the pyramid of Maslow's hierarchy of needs.

First you met your physiological needs by putting food on the table, eventually earning enough in commissions to allay most feelings of scarcity and fear about the future. That base of happy customers helped to fill the need for love and belonging. Their admiration, coupled with respect from industry peers, creates the internal audience that shouts, "We've made it!" You've reached the second-highest tier on the pyramid: esteem.

Now, fast forward a year or two. Things feel different. Somehow you've managed to be frazzled and bored at the same time. The same transactional or business challenges that used to feel exhilarating now just frustrate you. You're tired of constantly reinventing the wheel when it comes to lead generation, and you've had it with wasting money on over-hyped technology solutions that don't deliver on their promises.

Those exhausting sessions with your accountant and bookkeeper seem ever more frequent and taxing. You are unsure what the problem is, but certain that you are not fulfilling your potential. You silently wonder, "There has to be a better way . . . right?" The top level of Maslow's pyramid, self-actualization, seems unreachable.

Somehow you've managed to be frazzled and bored at the same time.

Right now and all across the country, thousands of other agents are banging their heads against the same ceiling. Don't get me wrong; there is a well-worn path to success that involves producing at a high level and gradually shifting your focus from selling to sponsoring sales agents. But progress is slow-going, and the road to business ownership is littered with the bodies of burnout cases who sabotaged their own careers after years of frustration. For most agents, transitioning out of personal production in the traditional model is a 10- to 20-year proposition. After one or two decades of writing contracts until midnight, trading school plays for property showings and the stress of handling one transactional dumpster fire after another, broker-owners can lose their passion for the business. Frankly, they start to resent their clients right along with the sales agents. What they've built are shops that are big and slow, with a daily grind that bears little or no resemblance to the fun, exciting days of their early careers.

Believe me when I say that this doesn't have to be you. I know from experience.

My name is Chris Watters, and through trial and error I've discovered a way to QUICKLY scale the team model and gain massive market share in just three years.

Let me rewind a bit and tell you how we got here.

I entered the real estate industry in late 2006, as an overconfident new college grad who had it all figured out. With the ink still wet on my new degree in finance, I thought I could do no wrong. I started my career on a team under a big-box broker, leveraged the hot market to create some quick success, and closed a ton of deals in the span of just a few months. In the first few months, I was totally entrenched in reading books and attending

> *Foolishly, I viewed these early victories as proof of my financial invincibility.*

continuing-ed classes. Despite grinding out a handful of deals early on, I quickly realized the team I was on didn't have enough opportunities to help me grow as fast as I wanted. At the ripe age of 22, I lacked the patience and humility to stay focused and wait for a better opportunity in the real estate industry. So, after only four months, I jumped ship and essentially exited the real estate industry.

In 2007, the Texas energy market was booming! I decided to use my new real estate skills to help energy companies locate the owners of mineral rights and negotiate oil and gas leases. Again, the new venture ignited and I was in the money. The outlook for my career couldn't have been more positive.

Foolishly, I viewed these early victories as proof of my financial invincibility. In December of 2008, the Texas energy market crashed. The price of natural gas and oil plummeted. The major energy conglomerate that had contracted my services laid off over 1000 people before the year was up. I was one of them.

When I heard the news, the instant relief I felt just confirmed that the layoff was a blessing in disguise. Truthfully, I hated the job. So, for my next move, I decided to take all of my savings and open up a bar and restaurant in downtown Austin. The business thrived . . . until the economy collapsed in the summer of 2009. Our bread and butter consisted of corporate events, and overnight those budgets all dried up at once. I was out of business by the fall of 2009.

> *I literally lost it all.*

I literally lost it all. I had accumulated my savings over the years from various sources: selling homes for those few months, the oil and gas leasing, money I pocketed from selling my lawn mowing business, AND the profit I received from the sale of my first home, which I purchased while in college. All that time I had lived meagerly, pinching pennies to amass what was a small fortune for someone my age.

It's tough to keep the cocky bastard mentality going when you're sleeping on your girlfriend's couch and watching your life savings go up in flames. It sounds trite, but now I'm truly grateful for the experience because it taught me that absolutely nothing is guaranteed. Things can change in an instant, and we have to be prepared.

I wrote this book because in 2011 I found myself building my own real estate Death Star.

I wasted so many years with distractions and falling on my face in industries that I had no passion for. I thought back to when I was the happiest in my professional life. What was the one opportunity that challenged me but didn't feel like "work"? The entire time I was in the oil and gas industry AND during the bar and restaurant venture, I had always wanted back into real estate. I had kept my sales license active although I wasn't actively selling homes. That allowed me to sit for the broker's exam. (The requirements for getting your real estate broker's license were super lax at the time.)

I opened Watters International Realty in the summer of 2010. The seemingly grandiose company name was a head-scratcher for my friends and family, but I was pigheadedly determined to succeed at an extreme level. I was inspired by other entrepreneurs who added the word *international* to their company names to help lend credibility to their ambitious plans. Not to mention, I loved the idea of traveling the globe to help people find a better path to success in the real estate industry.

In hindsight, I realize that the company name was my way of "burning my ships." If you've never heard that phrase before, it refers to conquerors who landed on distant shores, setting their boats aflame, as if to say to themselves, "Retreat is not an option." Still, the name must have sounded funny to anyone walking into my first office, which was about as big as a queen-size bed.

I built a team, we made lots of money, and the rest is history — right?

No. Not even close. This brings us back to the problem of building a team under the traditional real estate brokerage model.

I wrote this book because in 2011 I found myself building my own real estate Death Star. I hired a ton of agents. Constructed using the traditional broker/agent model, the whole business revolved around me. In this hub-and-spoke setup, the agents depended on me alone for their broad array of needs. Given that they were at wildly different experience levels, my days were spent spinning my wheels, in reactive mode. If I didn't make the decision, no decision was made.

So I burned it all down.

And, through some high-intensity experimentation, I built a machine of a brokerage that produced $3.1M in GCI in the first 3.5 years, netting over $1M in pretax profits on an average sale price of $225k. By reinvesting the vast majority of profit back into the company and testing big initiatives in advertising and back-end systems, I was able to also create the first and only model designed to help agents quickly build their own team-centric brokerages.

Contained within these pages are the keys to creating an exceptionally profitable, quickly scalable model that creates raving-fan clients and empowers rockstar salespeople. Read on and you'll get this tactical advice:

WHAT YOU'LL LEARN

- Where not to waste your advertising dollars
- How to affordably create thousands of buyer leads
- How to recruit, train, and retain agents and staff
- What positions to create and in what order to fill them
- How to grow leaders within your organization
- How to build a single technology solution that works with all departments
- How to measure success for each role within your company
- How to leverage vendors to pay for your advertising
- How to open your first brick-and-mortar office for next to nothing

I have paid the tuition for all of these lessons so you don't have to.

Most importantly, you'll learn how to move from a management mentality to a mindset of ownership. The beauty of building out the team model is that the business doesn't all depend on you. At some point, your presence in the office could even become an unnecessary distraction for your team.

Reading that last sentence might feel a little threatening to those of us with giant egos, but think about it for a second. How many more years would you like to take calls from impatient sellers and stressed-out buyers at 10 p.m.? How many more dance recitals would you like to miss because "We're all gonna die if you don't revise my repair amendment RIGHT NOW"?

Consider this book a light at the end of the tunnel for your career, or more accurately, a wormhole that shaves a cool 15 years off your journey from agent to business owner. This strategy is the product of literally millions of dollars in experimentation on initiatives both failed and successful. Simply put, I have paid the tuition for all of these lessons so you don't have to.

Capitalize on the momentum and passion that you have right now, and build something amazing while you still can. But before we begin, I want you to really think about whether you're up to the challenge of creating Explosive Growth.

TURN TO THE FOLLOWING PAGE ONLY IF:
- You want to become a great leader.
- You want to build a team that succeeds without your constant attention.
- You're committed to saving money and reinvesting into your business.
- You're willing to work your tail off.

I want to make it clear that, unlike other real estate how-to books, this one is written from pure experience, not conjecture. Each section is based on doing, not on surveying other agents or speculating about what's possible under perfect conditions. Rather, the book is written using seven years' worth of practical application and testing. We ground it out the hard way, screwed it up left and right — until we failed our way to success.

If you want to know how I created over $1 million in net income after just three years, keep reading. On to Chapter 1!

CHAPTER 1
An Overview of the Seven Pillars

I've structured this book around three key phases of your team's development. I've named those stages the Early Climb, Awkward Teenager, and Explosive Growth. In each phase, I'm going to tell you exactly what to do to build and strengthen the seven key pillars of your business.

Every business succeeding at a high level MUST develop mastery of these areas. Otherwise, its growth is marked by long periods of stagnation or even stunted forever. Your new real estate team is no exception. The key pillars you're going to build are:

Now, it would be easy for me to dump all of this information on you at once and call it a day. Instead, I'm going to use the three phases of your team's development to walk you through the actions you must take at each stage. I recommend reading this book one time all the way through, and then focusing each phase to work through the items appropriate for that time. Let's start with a short overview of each pillar here, looking at what each of the fundamentals means to you now and to "future you" as you build out your lean, innovative, and exceptionally profitable team.

LEADERSHIP AND SCALING

I always say that for the first few years of my company's history, my job was mostly about driving a proverbial fire truck around all day long, extinguishing one smoldering pile of real estate after another. To get away from the day-to-day grind of supervising agency work, you're going to need some help. Lucky for you, you're about to learn how to recruit the right people and train them like you mean it. If you learn how to identify talent early, you'll be ahead of the curve in developing the future leadership of your company. Those folks absolutely hold the keys to scaling your business. Together we'll walk through the steps you'll take to build that leadership and scaling ladder that makes your Great Escape possible.

MARKETING AND LEAD GENERATION

Of course, if we had assembled all the other pillars in expert fashion but neglected marketing and lead generation, we would have been bankrupt in weeks. Building the ultimate real estate team by training agents and perfecting systems is completely pointless if you don't have reliable streams of new business coming in. I've seen real estate offices built that way, and their salespeople just become the best agents that nobody's ever heard of!

NOTHING happens without marketing and lead gen. Now that we've demonstrated my exceptional command of the obvious, let me qualify this by stating that we're going to be cramming a lot more than advertising knowledge into the these lessons. For your new team, getting the phone to ring is just the first step. Ignore the thousands of lead generation and advertising vendors out there vying for your ~~attention~~ money. I'll teach you the "broke ninja" marketing tactics to implement first, and how to know when you're ready to take your marketing to the next levels.

Ignore the thousands of lead generation and advertising vendors out there vying for your ~~attention~~ money.

TECHNOLOGY

The lead-gen conversation is a natural segue to our next pillar: technology. Marketing creates leads, which your team will convert into appointments using certain tech tools laid out in the coming chapters. Those deals turn into pending contracts, and managing those contracts demands other software tools. Those pendings turn into closings, and happy clients with whom we must communicate for life if we want to secure a steady flow of referrals. That requires (you guessed it!) more tech. I'll show you what systems to employ while staying within a budget that's right at each stage.

RECRUITMENT

Like marketing and lead generation, if we don't make recruitment a priority at each step, your growth will stagnate before you can say "ditch the gold jacket." You'll learn how to go from persuading agents to work with you to attracting mass numbers of agent candidates. Now that I think about it, this book really ought to come with a stick to beat back the crowds of agents who will want to be a part of your new team. You'll learn who to hire for what roles, and who to take a pass on.

COACHING AND TRAINING

What good is it to provide a ton of warm leads and killer systems if you're not also providing the coaching and training your team needs to extract all the juice from those investments? Don't reinvent the wheel every time you hire a new buyer agent or member of support staff. I'll show you how to create a repeatable system of onboarding, and how to train, motivate, and support your team on an ongoing basis without getting lost in the world of people management.

BACK OFFICE

Your growing team superstructure requires a solid foundation. Through trial and error, I've come up with a system of back office roles and processes that can be scaled to support the outer limits of what you can achieve — and without the bloated labor costs that kill profitability in rapidly expanding organizations like yours. From accounting to listing management, find out how to create a lean and highly productive operations team.

THE SECRET SAUCE: BRAND AMBASSADOR PROGRAM

You know what? I'm gonna go ahead and tell you, right this instant, the secret sauce that makes the Great Escape achievable on such a short timeline. I call it the brand ambassador program. I'll show you how to create strong vendor relationships early and how to get those vendors on board with cost-sharing some of your marketing initiatives. You'll take those initial partners and grow that team into a true business mastermind group that shares inside info (and leads!).

Growing your real estate team is like playing chess; you MUST have a strategy.

ASSUMPTIONS AND DISCLAIMER

This book is written under the assumption that you're going independent and are a broker yourself (or have a broker to sponsor your new operation) and that you will be responsible for creating the recipe for each department yourself. So, a quick disclaimer: Making the decision about whether to launch your team independently or under a franchise umbrella may impact the feasibility of one or more of my recommendations. Remember that while I'm trying to be as unambiguous as possible about how to achieve Explosive Growth, it's possible that the structure of your franchise agreement could keep you from fully implementing The Million Dollar Real Estate Team model.

HOW THIS BOOK IS ORGANIZED

Consider the Leadership and Scaling section of each chapter as a thousand-foot view of your business. Where are you now, and where are you headed? How do you know when to move forward with a new hire or when to fire yourself from one duty and give it to someone else? Growing your real estate team is like playing chess; you MUST have a strategy. In Leadership and Scaling, we'll zoom out so that you can see the whole board and what moves come next.

In other sections of this book, I'll give you the practical tools that you will need to make individual chess pieces move in the right direction. For example, the Recruitment and Hiring section of each chapter is super tactical, full of rich detail and action items for screening candidates and building your first team environment.

You'll notice that the Seven Pillars appear in a different order in each chapter. That's intentional, as a matter of practicality. For example, early on you have to get your technology ducks in a row before you move forward; in the middle stage you're going to build a solid back office foundation before you can address the other pillars.

Compared to you, the large brokerages are lumbering behemoths.

BEFORE WE BEGIN

Right now, you probably feel like you're standing at the foot of Mount Everest. Part of you wants to shy away from putting yourself out there, from all that responsibility. Maybe you've got a sudden urge to pick up a toddler-sized bag of Cheetos and hide under the blanket until I just go away. But if you're the agent I wrote this book for, your true self is excited by the growth potential and energized by the idea of reclaiming your life. New wheels are turning in your head; you're getting a taste of the mindset of a business owner versus that of a service practitioner.

Go ahead and address some of the limiting beliefs that you've created about starting your own company. You may be thinking that you'll never be able to compete against the big-box brokerage juggernauts. In reality, you have a slew of advantages because of your size. Your business is nimble; you can easily test things and pivot on a dime when they don't work. You can implement initiatives quickly and be agile in the marketplace. Compared to you, the large brokerages are lumbering behemoths. Making any significant course correction is a seven-figure, multi-year proposition.

Kick the idea of building a team around long enough, and the risk-averse committee living in your head will likely begin to argue that this is too much work, that you don't have what it takes to build a business. (And if you are fool enough to make an attempt, you'll certainly be forced to live out of a van and eat dog food, so it's best not to try.)

The choice is between listening to the committee or to your true self, the one who wants so much more than what you have now.

Who do you CHOOSE to believe?

CHAPTER 2
The Early Climb

In Early Climb, your focus is on taking massive action to set up the Seven Pillars as quickly as possible. Why the hurry? All of the extra "stuff" involved in starting a team can create a quagmire that kills production, so this boot-up period must be kept as brief as possible. Get bogged down in making your website perfect and you'll postpone your profitability. Take too long in setting up your first Brand Ambassadors, and you'll cut your lead-gen off at the knees. Let's do a quick overview of what you need to accomplish and when. (And, psst, check out our exclusive bonuses at bonus.wirbook.com like a sample launch calendar that you can download RIGHT NOW.)

LEADERSHIP & SCALING

In the end, what's going to make your team a giant success isn't the cutting-edge technology or effective marketing. It's the people. Building an amazing team, the 20% that yields 80% of results, comes down to your ability to find the right WHO. You'll start by making your first investments in people, growing your team, and delegating repetitive tasks and one-off projects that distract you from your dollar-productive activities. I'll show you how to structure your team in such a way that each player has a specialized role and gets "ninja good" at his or her short list of responsibilities.

Another key thrust involves cultivating strategic business partnerships that allow you to double or triple your lead-generation efforts. You might think that other businesses won't want to market with you until you've proven your new team concept, but my teams have proven again and again that this limiting belief is unfounded.

Creating an excess of inbound leads will be important when you're building your sales team and need to incentivize agents to join your group. An ongoing recruitment effort aimed at onboarding two to four buyer agents a month will help you scale now and in the future. The sales team is the ideal proving ground for the future leaders of your company.

If you're successful at recruiting, you'll find yourself needing to train and coach your new sales team. I'll show you how to systematize your training and leverage coaching resources to help you create successful launches for your agents while leaving time for your other responsibilities.

You can't really build and train a team from your home office, so it's going to be important to secure a brick-and-mortar workspace. I'll show you how to create a client-friendly, professional working environment on the cheap and with very flexible terms.

But first things first.

Who Are You?

Deciding that you're ready start a company is half the battle. But what kind of business do you want to build? What's your culture? What are your standards? What do you want the public to think of when they hear your company name?

> **Before you lay the foundation of your enterprise, answer three questions:**
>
> - What is our mission?
> - What is our vision?
> - What are our core values?

I get it; at this point you're already a little overwhelmed, anticipating the million practical decisions to be made when starting a one-person empire. Questions like these might seem a little "woo-woo" when you're consumed with googling more practical things like "where to buy used office furniture." But determining your company's foundational DNA is crucial, and it deserves thoughtful consideration.

Consider this analogy from real estate sales: If you've ever seen a home with foundation problems, you know that mistakes made in the very beginning of the construction process can have catastrophic effects on all areas of the home's performance over time. If the slab cracks, so will the plumbing lines. Tiles break, roof joists twist out of square, and cracks trace the walls. Doors and windows don't open and close like they should. Poor preparation and corners cut at the start of construction are often to blame.

So goes your business if you don't model it upon a sound set of principles that align with your own core values. You are the business owner now; this is your ark to build how you want it. Design it with care and precision. An initially flawed concept can render years of unnecessary struggle and frustration.

You are the business owner now; this is your ark to build how you want it.

Get Strategic

A thoughtful strategic planning process can help you think through the important questions that must be answered before starting a new organization. Good strategic planning is more than just listing the objectives you'd like to accomplish. The process will help you think through what you're really trying to achieve when it comes to hard goals (like production volume) and soft goals (like company culture).

Let's go over the key items to flesh out in the first part of your strategic planning:

Mission: What are the results that you want to create now? Consider the possible dimensions here. You could think about mission in terms of client outcomes, opportunities created for your team, or maybe ways that your business will differ from the brokerage next door.

Vision: Where is your company heading? What's the end goal for your business? If you are successful in executing your mission over time, what does your organization look like in five or ten years?

Core Values: What are the guiding principles that determine how you and your team make decisions? Your company's core values should align with your own. If you value creating home-run experiences for your clients over a "just get the deal done" attitude, then build that into your company from the start.

Brainstorm words and concepts that come to mind when you think about your own values. It's more important that the words resonate with you than it is that they look good on paper or sound slick.

As an example, here are our company's core values. This poster hangs on the wall in our offices:

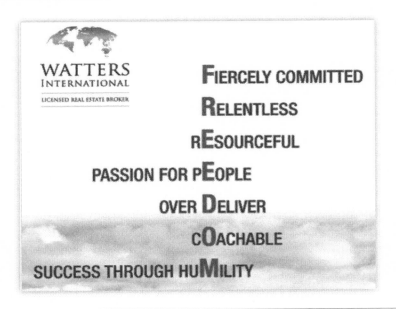

Our values are not especially catchy; but each one represents a vital ingredient in our recipe for success. Behind every one of those words are stories about wrestling tough transactions to the ground, helping agents push past their limitations, and delivering crazy levels of services that no other broker would have.

We came by this list through years of discussion. To be honest, the mistake we made early on was not spending enough time getting these right on Day 1. (Thus, we hired a bunch of bad eggs.) Along the way, we realized that our individual values were all moving toward the same overarching concept: freedom. Freedom from debt, from scarcity and insecurity — all of those are the byproducts of walking the walk of coachability, passion for people, etc. Freedom to design your career how you want it is within reach, as is the freedom to travel the world or make a difference. We've built our business around creating that freedom of choice. You'll see this phrase come up again and again when we look ahead to your Great Escape.

As our company evolved over time, so did our values. It's OK if yours do too. Adding more team members will provide more insights on who you all are as a company. You learn lessons together that help to sharpen your understanding of those principles that guide you.

If your values align with the needs of the consumer and you practice them faithfully, you're going to experience success and profitability. For now, this is yours in total to design and deserves serious consideration.

SWOT Analysis

The second part of your strategic planning is a classic SWOT analysis. Not familiar? A SWOT analysis involves assessing your business on its strengths, weaknesses, opportunities, and threats. This technique has been around for more than half a century and holds up as well today as it did fifty years ago. The assessment helps you, the owner, get a better handle on your position in the market.

It is crucial that you complete a thorough analysis of your business in each of these categories before you decide what your true objectives should be and the priority for each. Let's go over the different categories:

SWOT ANALYSIS

- **Strengths:** What are the resources you have at your disposal that will help you to succeed? Where are your competencies? What personal attributes do you possess that help create success? If you already have a small team, what additional abilities or qualities do they have that will surely create forward momentum for your business? Who are the people already in your corner?

- **Weaknesses:** What are the internal flaws that you and your organization need to remedy if you're going to grow in the ways that you want? What are you doing that isn't working anymore? What are you inefficient at doing, and where are your incompetencies? Among the people in your life today, who is a drag on your success?

- **Opportunities:** Opportunities are different from strengths in that they are external. What are the conditions in the marketplace that you can take advantage of? What are the needs of consumers that you can capitalize on and that are currently going unmet? Who are the players that you could add to your team that would help you grow exponentially?

- **Threats:** Also external to your business, threats are the boogeymen that keep business owners awake at night. What outside events could negatively impact your company? What could the competition implement that would knock your company down a peg, or worse — make you obsolete altogether? Who are the people who mighty actively try to keep you from succeeding?

What should you do with this information? Keep it handy, as you are going to need it at the end of this chapter.

Structuring Your Team

As you dive into this book, you will soon notice that the fundamental structure of the team model is wildly different from that of a traditional, hub-and-spoke brokerage. The model I'm recommending to you here is built on the premise that specialized units of experts will deliver a more consistent experience for the consumer, more opportunity for the agents, and higher profit margins for the owner.

The traditional real estate model focuses on the single-operator, generalist agent. These agents work with both sellers and buyers, and may also offer property management or tenant representation services on the side.

On its face, this arrangement sounds versatile and efficient. However, buried within each of those real estate subcategories are wide variations in the skills and aptitudes required to expertly execute each type of service. The experience that allows us to anticipate unintended consequences, the ability to see around corners, and the confidence to take charge of complex situations and offer unambiguous guidance — all of that expertise comes only from learning through practice, not dabbling.

How to screw this up

If you want to screw up strategic planning, make it a completely pointless exercise, and leave the results in a drawer until it's time to update them next quarter. For example, in the first couple of years of my team's development, we didn't put a lot of thought into our core values. I basically came up with a set of principles that we generally believed in (and that sounded really good). One year I decided to approach it in a different way. Without any guidance, I asked my executive team to talk about the common threads that each of our top performers shared. The floodgates opened, and within minutes we had total clarity on what makes our team special. Our core values were posted on the walls and added to our new employee/agent training programs.

The day the core values really came alive was when we began actively using them to make decisions. When hiring or not hiring a new associate was debated, we brought out the core values. "Is this person Coachable? Do you see her being Fiercely Committed?" Using your core values as a compass turns complex, ambiguous decisions into no-brainers.

> *Specialization increases productivity, and productivity increases profitability.*

Repetition also breeds efficiency. A specialist will execute tasks not only with expertise and confidence but also with speed and the benefit of rote memory. Specialization increases productivity, and productivity increases profitability.

Buyer specialists work with buyers, while listing specialists work with sellers. Coordinators also specialize once your team hits Explosive Growth. I will show you how to link these three units together and build a cooperative where individual experts come together to create amazing results for each client.

Leadership in the Early Climb

There is an ocean of space between a great leader and a "boss." In the Early Climb, you'll set the tone for the style of leadership you're likely to deliver over the life of your company. You could choose to be any of these:

- **The Dictator:** You rule unilaterally, with little or no explanation of why you do things the way you do. The team sees you as a stubborn jerk who doesn't appreciate their contributions.

- **The Professor:** Wanting to please everyone, you over-research and seek consensus on every weighty decision. The team perceives you as weak and ineffectual.

- **The Visionary:** Bold, fearless, and willing to pivot on a dime, you inspire some with your big ideas and terrify others with your constant changes. You'll make loyalists out of the team members who can survive the professional whiplash you leave in your wake.

- **The Ostrich:** When faced with a challenging situation, you creatively avoid the problem in hopes it will go away on its own or be solved by someone else. Talented players don't stick around the ostrich very long.

These are natural leadership styles. They are the products of diving head first into management without giving much thought to what kind of leader you really want to be.

To effectively direct your real estate operation, you will need to adopt a style that is more intentional. Consider the problem that we're trying to solve. Let's think through the constraints and challenges of leading a team in the Early Climb:

> Regarding your wage-earning employees, you don't have enough cash reserves to hire the wrong person, have him or her not work out, hire/train again, and repeat. You must be incredibly thorough in vetting your candidate and fire early if the relationship is not igniting.

> The buyer agents who are willing to take a chance on you when you're in your Early Climb are likely to be of the brand-new and high-needs varieties. They may be afraid of rejection and have problems with outbound prospecting. They may fudge their call numbers and retreat into busy-work to avoid challenging tasks.

> You can hire very experienced agents, but the real estate industry at large has likely ruined them from being able to appreciate and follow a more structured program. After years of working from home and reporting to no one, many agents are not able to be retrained to operate within a professional environment with high expectations.

> Managing people is only one hat that you'll wear, and it's much harder to be consistent and firm in your leadership when you're exhausted by the 12-hour days of real estate whack-a-mole. Arranging appointments, training agents, and interviewing assistants can bring out the Ostrich leader in all of us.

What kind of leadership does a business with these conditions need? What type of approach will allow you to shore up the weak spots and help amplify the strengths?

Make the decision to set aside your natural management style. Fix your intention to be the leader that your business deserves.

LESSONS I'VE LEARNED THE HARD WAY:

- **Set expectations clearly and set them early.** Tell all new hires what success looks like and how you—and they—will know things aren't working out. State the expected results and necessary timeline simply, and ask the associate to repeat those things back to you. Leave every hire with a one-page list of your requirements and a plan for success. In writing, communicate the areas where the associate has total discretion, which elements require your consultation, and which ones they should never touch with a ten-foot pole.

- **Hit the ground running.** Create a checklist of the tools the associate needs to succeed. Communicate in advance any resources that you'll require the associate to provide, such as a laptop and MLS access for a buyer agent. For the items that you must provide, make sure all those items are set up and tested before that person's first day on the job.

- **Give feedback early and often.** Most of your associates will possess no psychic abilities, so you owe it to them to let them know how they're doing. Don't withhold praise. Many of us assume that our team members know that we think they're doing a great job. They usually do not. Make sure that negative feedback given verbally is followed up with a summary email so that you have a record of your corrective guidance in case you wind up in an unemployment dispute.

- **Show them the big picture.** Leadership, if boiled down to its essence, starts with the ability to get people to buy into your vision. As the rainmaker, you must regularly communicate your core values and your vision. As a leader, you should have the goal of helping your team understand that they're working on something that's greater than themselves. Creating a culture that ties every important decision back to its core values has to be woven into the foundational DNA of your company.

- **Consider unintended consequences.** Every decision you make really needs to be considered in terms of the potential effect on each department. You will be faced with tough choices; in fact, in Early Climb they seem to come by the dozen, and you will not have the luxury of indecisiveness. Your ability to assess a situation and make a quick business decision will determine the pace at which your organization evolves.

Speaking of leadership — you probably understand the need to arrange your pillars to successfully launch your new team. But what's not super-apparent is that you're actually laying the groundwork for the future leadership of your organization. Hire the right executive assistant and you could've just found your future COO or CFO. A key thrust to move you into the next stage of growth will be identifying and grooming a buyer agent team leader; if all of your early agent hires are duds, you can't move into the next phase.

A how-to book for the traditional real estate model would tell you to get a mentor at this point. But a broker/agent who thrived in a traditional big-box brokerage model is almost guaranteed not to understand this path to success (and certainly will not be able to offer you much advice along the way). For those of you who do not want to go it alone, make sure you check out the conclusion, where we talk about ways to get help along your journey.

Ready to get granular? Let's take a dive into the details of your first impact zone: the early technology that makes everything else possible.

TECHNOLOGY

OK, so the technology piece isn't your favorite. Relax. I'm about to lay out a plan to implement the important systems without losing momentum or wasting money. I've put together a list of essential services that are inexpensive and relatively easy to set up. These selections are good bets when it comes to paying for themselves in the first year.

Don't spend more than two days getting these systems up and running. The top priorities are the ones that directly put dollars in your pocket. If your website isn't exactly perfect after a couple days of setup, just roll with it. You'll tweak things as you go.

Here's the short list of systems that need to go live before turning up the volume on your recruitment and marketing, along with cost estimates on each item:

Systems and Costs

- Call-capture system to boost phone leads ($800 startup, $200/month)

The Early Climb

- Phone campaign tracking and recording ($50/month)
- A basic property search site with back-end lead management ($700 startup, $200/month)
- Virtual tour and photo engine for listings ($50/month)
- Speed-dialer licenses ($0 startup, $150/month per license)
- Hiring software ($25 to $100/month)
- Gmail and Facebook accounts (Free)
- YouTube account (Free)
- GroupMe or Slack (Free for now)
- Payroll software ($50/month)

Disclaimer: *We may be able to negotiate preferred pricing for persons whom we refer to these vendors, and/or we may receive compensation that helps us keep the price of this book low. However, we recommend ONLY our favorite vendors and will continue to recommend them even if they don't have an affiliate program in place. In some categories there is only one vendor with whom we have experience and whom we can recommend; in others, where there are two comparable systems we like, we recommend both systems.*

Call-capture Systems

If you've never used one before, a call-capture system (commonly referred to as IVR or MVR, for reasons that don't really matter) is typically built around a call to action that prompts clients to call a 1-800 number and enter a four digit code for recorded line info on the subject property. Depending on the vendor, your agents may receive a text or an email with the caller's phone number so that the agent can immediately call them to book an appointment. Newer systems also offer a feature that causes the caller to be connected directly with an agent after the recorded message. Call-capture systems are incredibly effective for creating mass numbers of phone leads. For every call that your agents receive from the phone number on the main for-sale sign, expect to receive at least three times that number via the call-capture system.

> *Pro tip for results with the MVR system: best practices dictate that you not include the list price in the recorded presentation, on your flyers, or in your Craigslist ads.*

I recommend you check out Proquest Technologies' MVR Marketing Suite[1] for your initial call-capture system. (You may want to move to the more feature-rich Voicepad system down the road, but the emphasis at this stage is to employ the lowest-cost option with the greatest return.) The 1-800 number returns the highest number of leads when advertised on a sign rider posted on top of the flyer box, as well as on the flyers themselves. You'll also want to use the 1-800 number in your call to action in your Craigslist ads and other marketing pieces. The Proquest system even has a way to track which marketing avenue is delivering the results. Pro tip for results with the MVR system: best practices dictate that you not include the list price in the recorded presentation, on your flyers, or in your Craigslist ads. You don't want prospects to disqualify a property before you have a chance to speak with them. Expect to spend about $200 per month for the MVR service and an upfront expense of setup fee plus the cost of printing individually numbered sign riders.

New buyer agents may object to using MVR calls, as being connected to a live agent after the presentation can frustrate or annoy some prospects. This is a natural objection for agents new to the real estate business, but if the resistance persists after using the system for a while, it's a good indication that the buyer agent is not the right fit for your team of future top producers.

Phone Lead Tracking and Recording

In the team model, we have a separate buyer specialist team that operates apart from the listing team (and we'll explain why a little later). But for now, know that this separation requires that all listing signs and marketing

---

[1] During the Early Climb, you'll make a slew of decisions about what vendors and technologies to use. The products and services mentioned in this book are products that we have used in the past (many of which we continue to use, while others we have outgrown).

point toward centralized numbers that route to the buyer agent team. In the Early Climb, you can't expect calls to be handled as expertly as if you were answering them yourself; but there's no shortcutting this learning curve.

However, you don't have to blindly trust that your agents aren't giving bad advice or incorrect information to these extremely valuable warm leads. Instead, you're going to employ a clever, flexible (and affordable) tool to record the calls and have them emailed to you as .WAV files. I'm crazy about CallRail for this purpose. CallRail lets you easily obtain new local numbers so that you can track the results from campaigns like signs, third-party sites and your property search site. The interface is slick and intuitive to use, and it's very inexpensive.

Another very comparable tool is called Teletracker. At the time of this writing, its interface is a little less straightforward than CallRail's, but the system is feature-rich and allows for sending recorded calls to the agents along with your notes about the conversations.

Property Search Site and Lead Management System

Now that your call-capture system is in place and ready to produce loads of phone leads, take time to think through what to do with those leads once you create them. You'll need to invest in a scalable property search site and a lead management system (LMS). There are multiple vendors who offer both in the same package, but RealGeeks (rg.wirbook.com) is the current segment leader in terms of value and versatility. Their simple template sites are straightforward and easy to manage, and the open interface with other applications makes the platform a smart choice for businesses poised to one day outgrow their early systems.

The property search site will perform a variety of functions, including hosting lead capture pages for sellers, Contact Us forms, and other standard real estate website fare. But the tasks that it needs to perform flawlessly are the property search functionality and the automated email drips of listings relevant to the prospects' saved search criteria. Sometimes referred to as e-alerts, these emails are sent regularly (preferably daily) and are the key to maintaining prospects' engagement on your site.

Consistent re-engagement with the website increase the chances that you'll be top of mind when it comes time for the prospects to choose an agent. Expect to spend roughly $200 per month on a search site and LMS, keeping in mind that other vendors with more sophisticated systems are several times the price (often more like $1500 per month).

In the beginning, the leads will largely be input by the agents taking calls from the 1-800 call-capture service, along with some leads auto-imported from web sources like Zillow, Trulia, Realtor.com, Facebook, and Google AdWords. There's a cottage industry set up to sell search engine optimization (SEO) services to real estate agents. SEO development can be expensive and usually renders far fewer leads than the sources I recommend here. SEO work is not an expense I recommend in the early days of building your team.

Virtual Tour and Syndication Engine

One behind-the-scenes system that bears mentioning is a program that supports your marketing efforts in a few ways. There some great packages out there for creating flyers, hosting slick virtual tours, and syndicating listings across some of the multitude of real estate sites that may not pick up a feed from your local MLS. Our favorite is TourFactory because of its reasonable pricing and feature-rich environment. The system can handle many of the ancillary tasks involved in pushing a listing in front of as many sets of eyeballs as possible.

TourFactory can also convert your virtual tours to branded videos and upload them to YouTube. Social media posting is automatable as well. And it will send your seller reports about how many clicks the tours and postings get. Pretty cool, right?

Speed Dialers

If you've never used a speed dialer before, you've been missing out! Speed dialers are computer software programs that allow you and your agents to work much more efficiently by tightening up the time between prospecting calls (since the computer can dial numbers much faster than a person can). The dialer program may work with your existing cell phone or give you the option to dial directly from the computer using a "softphone." There are a few different products out there, some of them stronger in some areas than others. Vulcan7 is the probably the most versatile and useful for the team just starting out. Another tool, Mojo, is more of a pure dialer with some additional data services, such as like providing phone numbers for neighborhood prospection. On the other end of the spectrum, RedX is more adept at identifying leads to call but requires an additional purchase for dialer functionality. As the rainmaker, you should expect to be the primary user of the dialer software. As you expand, though, you'll increasingly be delegating this to others.

One quick note: remember to check all applicable laws about phone prospecting before using one of these products, as different jurisdictions may have rules and prohibitions about autodialers. Most autodialer products can filter out people on the Do Not Call Registry.

Hiring Software

You'll want to standardize your job-posting and applicant-screening process with a hiring tool that can grow with you over time. I recommend you check out a hiring software platform like HiringThing. This product can post job ads, send automated emails with links (we use that feature to send out a personality assessment), track the stages of the interview process, and report on which advertising sources are producing the most candidates. Additionally, the system produces cut-and-paste embeddable code for your website that helps you keep your Careers page current, based on the positions showing as available in your platform.

Google and Facebook

I recommend committing to the Google environment for all the basic tasks like email, calendar, file storage, web conferencing — you name it. Google's platform integrates better than anything else on the market. Use the free accounts at this stage in your development; later you can upgrade to the very affordable, professional Google Apps service that allows you to keep a copy of all emails sent from your server.

Yes, it does look more professional and credible if you have your own domain as the root for your email addresses. I have a solution to make this happen easily for free. You can easily work with website provider to create some vanity forwarders for your team's email accounts. It's usually free to mask your emails with a professional-looking email address, such as name@wattersinternational.com, which will forward to a free account like wattersteam.name@gmail.com. If you want to take things a step further, Gmail has a free (but somewhat complicated) procedure to mask your outbound emails with your vanity email address as well. I suggest prescribing an email address format for new agents, such as teamname.adam.s@gmail.com.

Facebook is used only in limited scope at this stage. You will want the agents to have the ability to quickly reach their sphere, promote their agent services, and share your company listings, open houses, etc. Later on, Facebook will come in handy as a lead-generation tool.

YouTube

You'll need to start a company YouTube account for hosting your virtual tour videos, but YouTube also makes a great platform for all of your visual marketing collateral because everyone trusts and knows how to use the site. In addition to your listing videos, you're going to send video emails to your database as part of your crusade for top-of-mind awareness.

If you've never poked around on the back end of YouTube, you may be surprised when you see the flexibility and functionality that this free service offers. You can host a live feed or special video event, or post clips that are private to you and your team. YouTube can take giant files and crunch them down to streamable size with ease, and it offers basic video editing capability as well.

Internal Chatter

One tech item that is super-easy (and free) to set up is a group texting app like GroupMe or Slack. Slack is the slicker option, but I've found GroupMe's free service to be incredibly solid. (I actually can't remember the system ever asking me to upgrade to a paid version.) As you build your team, you can create different groups on either of these apps, so your buyer agents can talk to one another while your listing team has a quick way to reach their cohort if need be. Or you can create a group of mortgage loan officers on GroupMe to quickly ask who is available for an over-the-phone loan application when you have a hot prospect on the line.

Accidentally, I discovered the morale-boosting power of these apps when I began to celebrate each new contract execution on the group text. It's really energizing for a buyer agent to get an instant "Way to go!" when he or she secures a new deal! Seeing your colleagues succeed in real-time can help foster a bit of healthy competition as well.

> *It's really energizing for a buyer agent to get an instant "Way to go!" when he or she secures a new deal.*

Payroll Software

I'd recommend that you set an expectation very early on that your company pays out twice a month; direct deposits are made on the 1st and 15th, whether you're a 1099 contractor agent or a W-2 employee. Since you're going to be performing payroll tasks in the Early Climb stage, you want to be able to batch these tasks into biweekly intervals instead of cutting individual checks every time an agent closes a deal.

You need software to streamline the payroll process. It may seem like an unnecessary spend right now, but think about the varying splits, commission rates, and fees that agents earn and/or pay. Calculating those totals by hand every two weeks is a huge timesuck. You'll thank yourself when it comes to tax time as well, as the system makes the tasks of creating 1099s and W-2s much simpler for your bookkeeper, which by itself saves you enough money to justify the expense.

We use ADP. Not only does it offer payroll services, there are additional features like managing 401k, health insurance, and HR compliance. Since

ADP is used by businesses large and small, it grows with you based on your organizational needs.

BRAND AMBASSADOR PROGRAM

Scaling your business quickly is going to require cash. Leveraging help from a network of partners is key to creating a quick bounce of new business in your Early Climb.

In this section, I'll teach you to hit up people you may or may not know for money. (OK, so that's a little oversimplified.) But you should know that this is essentially the goal, and it's a thousand times easier than it sounds.

First, the Why

Part of transitioning from a real estate practitioner to a business owner is learning your numbers. There are a few indicators that you really must keep a handle on, and we're going to go over two of them now.

Let's think about how you've gotten your leads thus far. Then we're going to figure out your lead acquisition cost and client acquisition cost.

"But Chris, most of my deals come from calling my sphere, or they are referrals from past clients. I don't have a lead cost or a client acquisition cost." I understand that, and, also, you're wrong.

Allow me to demonstrate:

Let's assume for the sake of argument that you are an agent who produced $100k in gross commission income (GCI) last year. If you're doing 30 transaction sides to get there, that's an average paycheck of $3333.00 per deal. Let's also assume that your business is 100% from sphere and past client referrals, and that you close one out of every two leads provided by your sphere and past clients.

To close 30 unique past client and sphere referrals in a 12-month period, I'm going to estimate that you are spending roughly two hours per day on telephone prospecting, sending blast emails, Facebook messages, and other creative means of engaging your database. At $100k in GCI for the year, I'm going to estimate that you're probably working about 50 hours per week on average, 50 weeks out of the year. That leaves us with 2500 working hours per year and makes your effective hourly rate $40.00, right?

Subtract the weekends and vacation days and we're left with 246 business days in the year. Divide that by your 30 closings and the calculator tells us that you create a new closed client every 8.2 days of prospecting. Remember that you're prospecting two hours each day, so now you have put in 16.4 hours at $40/hour to get that client. So, your client acquisition cost is actually $656.00, which my calculator says is much different than "free."

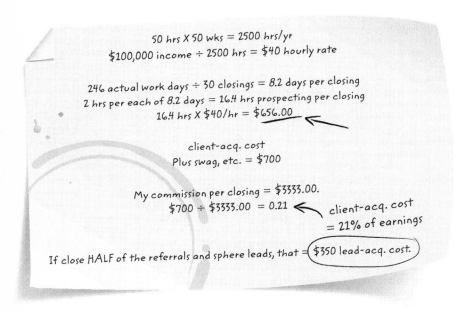

50 hrs X 50 wks = 2500 hrs/yr
$100,000 income ÷ 2500 hrs = $40 hourly rate

246 actual work days ÷ 30 closings = 8.2 days per closing
2 hrs per each of 8.2 days = 16.4 hrs prospecting per closing
16.4 hrs X $40/hr = $656.00

client-acq. cost
Plus swag, etc. = $700

My commission per closing = $3333.00.
$700 ÷ $3333.00 = 0.21   client-acq. cost
= 21% of earnings

If close HALF of the referrals and sphere leads, that = $350 lead-acq. cost.

If you're priming the referral pump with expensive items like closing gifts, pop-by giveaways, Christmas card mailers, recipe postcards, etc., we can conservatively round up to a $700.00 client acquisition cost, or 21% of your $3333.00 commission. If you close half of the referrals and sphere leads you receive, then that makes your lead acquisition cost $350.00.

You're probably wondering, "Why the math lesson?"

What I want to demonstrate here is the fact that as an agent, you are doing 100% of the heavy lifting when it comes to the efforts and expenses involved in creating new business. Now, think of all the companies and individuals downstream from you, who benefit from your giving up 21% of your commission each time you refer clients to them. Here are a few off the top of my head:

DOWNSTREAM VENDORS

- Lender
- Title company
- Insurance agent
- Custom builder
- Real estate attorney
- Roofer
- Plumber
- Electrician
- Cleaning service

Did you know there's a study that shows for every two homes sold, a job is created? In fact, NAR used data from 2010 to estimate that, on a median (at the time) home purchase price of $173,000.00, the total contribution to the Gross Domestic Product was $58,529.00.

Now, think about how much each one of those vendors has contributed to your marketing budget. If you're like the vast majority of agents, your vendors haven't contributed to your marketing at all. The closest thing to a co-marketing investment you can think of is that time the home warranty rep took you to Chili's.

Why should you be the only person spending money and time on developing new lines of business? Why should you bear all of the financial risk if an advertising campaign doesn't work out? To be clear, I'm not saying that these vendors are freeloaders. Every agent knows the tremendous value in having a ninja lender, and that excellent repair vendors regularly save the day on bumpy transactions. What I'm asking is, how equitable is this setup?

How to Secure Partners (and Deliver Results)

Now, before you get riled up about the injustice of it all, you need to own the fact that the main reason your vendors aren't contributing is because you haven't asked them to. Most of your trusted vendors are going to be willing to explore the idea of a monthly contribution in exchange for advertising services. Those services could include time during your team meetings to promote their businesses, advertising their services via blast email to your database, or hanging the vendors' promotional posters on the walls of your office for clients to see.

> The main reason your vendors aren't contributing is because you haven't asked them to.

In Early Climb, you're going to need to do some degree of convincing your vendor partners that they're getting in on the ground floor of something huge. Your team is headed for big things and you have a ton of momentum behind you. The limited number of eyeballs that you're able to get their name in front of today is just the beginning. Create a six-month agreement that details your advertising services and what each of them is worth. The short-term nature of this agreement feels more comfortable for the vendors and also sets the stage for increasing their contributions in proportion to the increased value you deliver over time.

Over time, the value to the vendors isn't just about receiving favorable positioning of their services by your real estate company. We'll address the future benefits in the next chapter.

We call this program the **brand ambassador program** (BAP) because it's a better representation of the reality of the relationship than just calling it a "vendor program." A brand ambassador is someone who is recommending services and also happens to have real credibility with a lot of potential customers. The credibility gives the brand ambassador influence needed to influence a potential customer. You and your team are ambassadors for these quality brands.

The reason that I've given the BAP top billing in this chapter is that if you knock this domino down first, it helps the others to fall more quickly. The BAP is essential to helping you scale your lead generation, and as we'll learn a little later, you're going to need leads to recruit buyer agents. The first vendors you reach out to are the service providers that you already know and trust. Add in anyone in your sphere who owns a well-run small or medium-sized business.

If you're a producing agent, you likely already have many of these relationships in place. The right vendor arrangements will add a boost to your lead-generation efforts and can produce secondary benefits like client referrals and introductions to new agent candidates. If you position this as an opportunity for your vendors and you to grow your lead-generation campaigns together, this becomes an all-around win/win relationship.

The next thing you'll do is to start with Google and create a list of the dream partners with whom you'd like to work. Respected roofers, handyman and cleaning service companies, and lawn-care providers are good examples. Take note of who is running Google AdWords campaigns to generate more leads (since that tells you that you're dealing with a company who is creatively trying to build more business). Another great resource is review sites like Angie's List and Yelp. Anyone who has excellent reviews is likely to be someone with whom you should align yourself.

Once you have your list built, you're going to start phone prospecting on those businesses. It's super important to make certain that you are getting to a decision-maker. Businesses get calls daily from marketing companies who promise the next big-hit solution, so most of them have at least an informal procedure in place for handling solicitation calls. You don't want to be lumped in with the advertising companies that are robo-dialing these businesses every day. You want to lead with the fact that you're a local real estate agent. Here's a good script to start:

Hi, my name is Chris Watters, with Watters International Realty. The reason for my call is that I was interested in meeting with whoever is in charge of your marketing or your Google and Yelp campaigns. I'm a local real estate agent, and it looks like you

guys are trying to grow your business, right? Well, I've got clients
who are constantly seeking people in the _____ industry, and
I don't currently have anyone to recommend. I'd really like to get
to know you guys personally and understand your business, and
maybe develop a relationship with you if it's a fit. When would
be a good time that I could sit down and meet the owner of the
company, or whoever heads the marketing department
or business development?

Sounds like a lot of work? These vendors don't just come knocking on their own accord. Get ready to juggle three key-pounding prospecting time blocks EVERY day! You'll be calling potential vendors, buyer agents, AND sellers.

Levels of Membership

Now that you've set the appointment, you have to create a value proposition that you offer to these vendors. Check out our Brand Ambassador Program promotional doc at bonus.wirbook.com. Our BAP has four different levels that range in cost. We have an entry-level program for $250 and more levels that increase in cost and value incrementally, from $500 to $1000. Then we have our platinum level, which is a customized package that can range from $2500 to an unlimited spend. There are only a few vendors who are going to apply for that. Companies that sell big-ticket items and consistently close your clients on their services should fall into that category. Mortgage companies and title providers may be good candidates for co-marketing on a large scale. It's imperative you maintain compliance with RESPA and other national and state laws. Providers of household services such as exterminators, roofers, and the like are more likely to see value in the $250 to $1000 range.

The $250 package, for example, gets the vendor's advertising on our custom guides for buyers and sellers, as well as on the vendor page of our website. We walk the clients through those buyer and seller guides in person and point out the brand ambassador's information. They also get onto our vendor list, which is what our agents and transaction coordinators use when sellers ask us for service referrals. We have a standing invitation for a monthly office visit from ambassadors, in case they want to present to our sales team or support staff. We also invite them to our client-appreciation events, which is a great place for the vendors to directly interact with past clients and each other.

The $1000 level comes with more services, including a video interview with the business owner that gets emailed to all the clients and leads in our giant database. We ask questions like "How did you get started? What separates you from the competition?" We really try to get down to the root of what makes the company special and why our clients should hire them. (I should point out that we only recommend vendors who are vetted and known for providing excellent service. This is a non-negotiable item.) We also ask questions to get the vendor to provide specific information that really helps educate the consumer. For example, when I interview a foundation repair company, I'll ask, "What can our clients do today to avoid needing foundation repair at all in the future? What's the difference between your company's warranty and the next guy's?"

When you're in the meeting with business owners, what's really important is to come from a very knowledgeable place when trying to get them to commit to working with you. It's just like working with a skeptical seller or buyer. Ask questions to understand the business and where its challenges are. You need to ask, "What do you do to drive traffic to your website? What are the ways that you generate the leads that turn into revenue? How much money do you spend to procure each client?"

We want to whittle down to that client-acquisition cost, because we need to make sure that the monthly subscription fee we're charging will deliver a positive return on investment for the vendor. For example, let's say that you're sitting across the table from a cleaning service that earns a profit of roughly $50 to $200 when they sign up a new customer. You're currently producing five deals per month as an agent. Even if they closed every one of your clients, they'd earn a max revenue of $1000. It makes no sense for them to enter into a $1000/month agreement with you, because you're not able to introduce them to enough people at this point for the partnership to be profitable. The $250/month program makes a lot more sense for this vendor. A goal is to create relationships early and grow them over time, not to sell vendors on something they don't need. Your approach should be very authentic and come from a place of genuinely wanting to help this vendor increase business and get a positive return on investment from the partnership.

You may be surprised by how many small and medium-sized business owners don't have a handle on some of their key indicators. It's not for lack of interest, but more about how successful service businesses often begin. Let's say that I'm a plumber and don't also happen to have an MBA. If I offer a great service at a good price, I will develop a set of loyal clients who, hopefully, refer like gangbusters. My business becomes prosperous, and advertisers take note, selling me on this marketing campaign or another. I hire more employees and am mostly consumed with managing people and growing the business. I know that the bottom line is healthy, but I'm not tracking the various lead sources and haven't a clue as to how to figure out what it costs me to obtain a new client.

If the vendor is unable to figure the client acquisition cost, then approach things from a less data-driven angle. Owners may not know what the actual cost is for each new customer, but they'll have a solid, off-the-cuff answer if you simply ask, "What are you OK with spending per client to get them to purchase your services?" He or she will know instinctively whether a $100 Google AdWords spend makes sense to procure a $500 job.

You know that you've done a great job demonstrating value when the prospect stops you mid-sentence and asks, "How much is all this going to cost me?" Once you have your partners all signed up, you will need to set up their payments. Nothing beats PayPal for ease of transfer, and the 3% processing fee can be passed along to the vendors as part of their agreements.

Demonstrating Value

When you're in Early Climb, it's challenging to deliver concrete results for your vendor partners right away. After all, you're just now building your team. As you build your buyer agent team and listing inventory, you'll quickly scale your pool of active buyers and number of buyer agent recruits. Getting your vendors in front of all of those people will result in more business generated for your partners.

The ideal brand ambassadors understand that they're investing in advertising now with an eye on long-term gains.

The ideal brand ambassadors understand that they're investing in advertising now with an eye on long-term gains. Still, most partners will want to see early proof that you're delivering on your promises.

How do you demonstrate value this early in the relationship? Here are a few tangible items that you can provide to show your partners that you're on top of things:

DEMONSTRATING VALUE

- **Produce an activity report for each vendor.** These reports should include the gross number of visitors to your website, as well as a copy of any blast emails that you have sent to your database that in any way advertise the vendor's services (even if it's just a hyperlinked logo placed below your email signature).

- **Invite them to present their services** to your first training classes of buyer agents.

- **Send screenshots of organic social media posts and paid advertisements** that you've produced that brag on the vendor's services.

- **Go through your vendor list each month and ask yourself, who in my sphere should this partner get to know?** It could be a past client who might need services in a few months, or a Facebook friend who mentioned off-hand that her lawn service isn't doing a great job. Err on the side of boldness; email them both and use a title like "John, Meet Sally." The body of your email could say something like "Sally, I was thinking about that HVAC unit of yours that's getting up there in age. You might want to talk to my friend John over at Honest John's AC Service. If anyone can squeeze another few years out of that thing, it's John!"

The bottom line is that you need to show the vendor partners that you're trying to help them get their money's worth, and then some. One other great way to add value is to hold a monthly "mastermind meeting" with the members of your BAP. This can help you identify potential sales people to join your team and will definitely be a boon to everyone invited. I'll go into detail more about this in the next chapter, but you could start connecting these partners with one another for a monthly meetup in the Early Climb if your BAP ignites earlier than expected.

 STAY INSIDE THE LINES

Be mindful of any federal, state, or local regulations that restrict what kind of agreement is allowable for each type of vendor. Non-settlement service providers are largely free to enter into any relationship as they want. (*Non-settlement* just means that these vendors are not involved in the settlement of the transaction; plumbers and roofers would qualify.) Lenders and title companies have the most restrictions, but they also have access to legal resources to make sure your partnership stays in compliance. Some vendors may want to verify the value of each benefit by using a third-party valuation company. So don't go crazy and wildly overvalue each item.

Don't do anything illegal. Make sure you are able to prove that your relationship is on the right side of the RESPA rules, state laws and the NAR Code of Ethics, should anyone hold a microscope to it. You may need to provide a disclosure to clients of any co-marketing relationship as well.

MARKETING & LEAD GENERATION

The most important pillar of business for any successful real estate brokerage to set up is marketing and lead generation. One of the core problems with the lone-wolf real estate brokerage model is the generalized nature of your role as rainmaker AND top producer. You are "Captain Everything," from the strategic (where to spend money, which audiences to target) to the granular (writing ads, testing campaigns). Most of us don't come from marketing or advertising backgrounds, and the dozens of other hats we have to wear don't allow us the luxury of becoming experts in these areas overnight.

> *One of the core problems with the lone-wolf real estate brokerage model is the generalized nature of your role as rainmaker AND top producer.*

Experimenting with advertising is an expensive proposition, one that is filled with risk. A plethora of opportunistic vendors exists who are more than happy to eat up your marketing budget with their flashy new (and often unproven) lead-generation products.

In the past five years I have spent, estimating conservatively, $5 million toward my team's advertising efforts. Some of them worked; many did not. Simply put, if you want to know what not to do with your marketing budget, I'm your guy.

We're about to dive into the bootstrapped, "broke ninja" marketing of the Early Climb. You'd better have those initial technology systems set up and the first brand ambassadors on board before you embark on this leg of the journey. No lazy steps!

Part I: Fishing for Buyers

In the pursuit of growth, your first hiring push as a new team leader will be to build a killer buyer agent team. (Don't panic. I'll detail for you in a later chapter how to recruit all of these agents.) But why do we have to build the buyer side first?

> *Building that killer buyer agent team will require you to make buyer lead generation your first area of focus.*

Remember that finding the right "who" is ultimately the one thing that makes your Great Escape possible. The incubator for most of those key operators is your buyer agent team. It's where you'll meet your raw talent and test their long-term potential for success on your team.

To build a good buyer agent team that operates at commission splits that allow your business to be profitable, you're going to have to supply the leads. Besides attracting great talent, these first leads are crucial for helping agents develop their scripting and conversion prowess.

But if you're doing roughly 30 deals a year, how do you supply enough leads to keep a buyer agent team fed? Let's assume that you're starting out with an average inventory of five listings or fewer at any given time. Organic leads on those listings are an unpredictable trickle and probably not enough to woo potential buyer agent candidates. Building that killer buyer agent team will require you to make buyer lead generation your first area of focus, while keeping the expenses low to protect your core capital goals, which we will establish later in this chapter.

Once your property search site and call-capture system are in place, I recommend using a few tried-and-true techniques to get more juice out of these systems before moving on to more expensive lead sources.

CREATING BUYER LEADS ON THE CHEAP

- Advertising other firms' listings (with permission, of course)
- Using amplified open house techniques
- Touching sphere and past clients via email, social media, and PHONE. (There is no replacement for a personalized phone call. This is the most undervalued and effective activity for maintaining relationships in a world where friends mainly communicate through social media.)
- Google AdWords
- Facebook ads
- Craigslist ads, utilizing call-capture service

Advertising Other Brokers' Listings

Research other firms in your service area that have listings but are weak on their internet marketing. Use the search bar on Craigslist to search the address numbers (or broker name, if your state requires that to be included in the ad). Figure out which brokers are not using Craigslist, and call them up for a friendly conversation.

Inquire about why they aren't they utilizing this tool. The answer is usually that they are behind the times on internet marketing or that they're

---

How to screw this up

I once had an agent give me permission over the phone to advertise her listings, only to call me a year later and read me the Riot Act for posting the ads. I reminded her about our conversation a year before, and she was cool — but I realized I hadn't followed up with her as I had promised. My buyer agents had been showing her properties like crazy, but any opportunity to expand the cooperation was lost because I didn't communicate the positive results. These advertising agreements must be in writing and you must keep the lines of communication open with the listing agent/broker.

simply too busy. Explain that you have a solution, and emphasize that your call-capture system will produce tons of Craigslist leads. Tell them you're confident that you can turn those inquiries into showings for their listings.

Ask for written permission to market their listings on Craigslist. Make sure that you follow the rules of your jurisdiction when it comes to how much of the listing broker's information needs to be disclosed in the ad (preferably far below your own contact information).

Amplified Open Houses

Now let's talk open houses. You're probably thinking "What's new about an open house?" and also "But I don't have many listings!" Keep reading. You can use the same technique above to find brokers willing to allow your team to hold open houses at their listings. Conventional wisdom would dictate that all brokers would want to keep those opportunities for themselves, but the fact is that open houses can feel like an exhausting distraction for experienced agents. At any given time, most agents usually have at least one anxious seller to satisfy, and providing open houses can be a way to appease a seller who doesn't understand that the chances of procuring a buyer for that particular property at an open house are next to nil. Create a win-win opportunity by holding the open house and using some ninja tactics to advertise it to increase chances of meeting an unrepresented buyer.

Here's a great sample script for that ask:

Hey Frank, my name is Chris Watters. I'm a local real estate agent in the area. I work for Watters International Realty. I noticed you've got this beautiful listing over at 123 Main St. I'd love the opportunity to hold that house open. If I get any buyers coming in I'll be sure to give you the showing feedback request forms with feedback from those buyers, which you can provide to your clients to add value. I will also be actively advertising the open house through door knocking, Craigslist advertising, and Facebook targeting [optional]. I'll promote your home to try to help you to get this listing sold faster. Is that something you'd be interested in?

For a very small budget, one amplified technique for promoting an open house is to run targeted Facebook ads to users who live within a one-mile radius of the subject property. You can use a picture of the home (again, with permission) as the main image and an attention-grabbing headline like "Want to see inside your neighbor's house?" This ad should cost less than $10 to run for two or three days.

Another tip for holding open houses is to have signs pre-printed with your company logo and directional arrows for guiding traffic through the neighborhood. Bright colors work best. Don't forget to order some signs with straight arrows to guide prospects down long stretches of road. Shop around and you'll find that custom-printed signs are often comparable in price to the stock open house signs sold by your local MLS association. Use a minimum of 12 directional signs to get those visitors to your open house. Put them out a few days before the open house for the best results.

A proven technique for increasing foot traffic at an open house is to door knock three days before the open house. Do it in the evening, when people are actually at home. Shoot for knocking on 100 doors and inviting them all to your open house. Hand each resident a property flyer (without the list price). If the invitation goes well, you can even ask the homeowner whether he has ever thought of selling his home, and offer to send him a monthly market snapshot email as a way to build your database. For those folks who provide their contact information, make sure to call them the morning of the open house to see if they're able to make it and whether or not they received the market snapshot.

A proven technique for increasing foot traffic at an open house is to door knock three days before the open house.

Here's a great script for your door-knocking sessions:

[KNOCK, KNOCK.]

Hi there! I'm Chris Watters of Watters International Realty and I'm doing an open house around the corner on Saturday and your neighbors told me to come over because I wanted to invite you. I'm going to have some cookies and coffee there and I'd love for you to come by. By the way, have you ever thought about selling your home? No? Well if you like, I'll send you a report so you know what's going on in the neighborhood. Would you like me to keep you up to speed on the home values in this neighborhood?

Agents who usually fear traditional door knocking for listings find this type of door knocking much more palatable, since it's harder for the occupant to be rude when you're inviting them to something. Expect to have about 20 to 30 conversations from knocking on 100 doors, and 5 to 10 of those will make it to the open house. The boost to foot traffic is huge, plus you've pre-built enough rapport that when they show up at the open house you're already past the "stranger danger" phase.

Meeting the homeowners is fun, and so is hosting a busy open house. The long-term benefit, though, lies in the addition of future sellers to your nurture database.

THE MOTHER OF ALL OPEN HOUSES

Open House

No open house produces results like a well-advertised afternoon at a foreclosure listing! A few years back we had some signs printed up that advertised "Bank Repo Open House" and offered a list of additional foreclosures in a tagline at the bottom of the sign. We were totally unprepared for the response!

So many people showed up to these events that we would lose count of the number of visitors that came through. In fact, one time we held an open house that literally caused traffic to back up in a neighborhood because of the number of people who poured in to take a peek.

People just can't resist the prospect of getting a below-market deal (or at least a peek at a foreclosed home). The foot traffic will be heavy, so my advice is to have your agents tag team these events with an outgoing mortgage loan officer who can help build rapport with as many visitors as possible. (This kind of assist is especially helpful for newer agents.) Play off of one another's strengths and you may find that your results are multiplied by having another professional in the room who speaks highly of your service.

Obviously these foreclosure open houses are harder to come by when the market is hot and bank repos are scarce. But they are still out there. Buddy up to the agents who have the contracts with asset managers to list and market the foreclosures. Make sure they know that you have professionally printed signs and that you'll get them a lot of traffic; bring them cake if you have to.

The list of additional foreclosures is digital-only. Do NOT keep paper copies with you. That way you can collect email addresses for all the folks who inquire.

The Right Way to Use Google AdWords

Google's pay-per-click advertising platform, called AdWords, sure gets a bad rap. I've heard many agents disparage the program because of its hefty price tag and the poor quality of the leads that it generates. But this is one lead source that literally delivers overnight and, if used strategically, can produce great results.

If you're not familiar with Google AdWords, take a second and head on over to Google.com. Type in "Dallas Homes for Sale." The top three or four search results, as well as the bottom two or three, all have a little icon beside them that simply says "Ad." That's your indicator that a company with something to sell has paid to place that ad on the Google search results (preferably on the first page).

Google makes money by charging the advertiser each time someone clicks on the ad. Keep in mind that a click is different than a lead. A click just gets the prospect to the second destination, which is your website. To convert to a lead, the prospect must go a step further and submit contact information. More of your clicks will result in aborted signups than will complete the form successfully. A majority of prospects leave the site after they're squeezed for info. Your percentage of users who don't complete the signup is called your **bounce rate**.

Google AdWords prices the clicks through a bidding system based on the popularity of keywords used in its users' search queries. This is the area where most realtors make a mistake in setting up their AdWords campaigns. If you're in the Dallas, Texas, real estate market and you create an ad to be shown when users type in "Dallas homes for sale" at peak times during the day, it's likely that hundreds of other agents are bidding on those exact same keywords. So the price goes way up, maybe $2.50 or more per click. Depending on the quality of your ad (and your website), you could need between 10 and 25 clicks to get someone to register as a lead. You could have a $60 cost per lead under those circumstances.

It gets worse. "Dallas homes for sale" is so broad that it's more likely that this ad would catch prospects early on in the consideration process. They're at least 6, probably 12 months out from purchasing. How do I know this? They haven't zeroed in on a neighborhood yet; otherwise, they would be using that neighborhood name in the search box instead of the very generic "Dallas homes for sale."

So what's a better way to implement an AdWords campaign? Go specific. Often referred to as "long-tailed" keywords, very specifically targeted ads can generate prospects who are further along in their contemplation of a home purchase. Examples: *Eanes ISD 1-story homes for sale. Houses for sale in*

Whispering Oaks, Austin. Condos in 78731 under 200k.

For most markets, the average ideal cost per lead is closer to $10, but you may have to go as high as $25 per lead if you're targeting areas with higher demand. In some mega-metros like the Bay Area, the cost per lead can range from $50 to $200 because the giant price points encourage fierce competition for these leads. Invest the time to find those keywords that produce affordable leads to fuel your Early Climb.

At this stage, you should be much more concerned with the quantity of leads, not the quality. Why? Because right now you need to show skeptical buyer agent candidates a LOT of leads that you need help handling. Plus, quality isn't so key at this stage because your buyer agents are just getting their feet under them when it comes to scripting and objection handling. Basically, your first agents are likely to be fairly new to the business, and new agents' phone skills tend to suck in the beginning.

New agents' phone skills tend to suck in the beginning.

If phone skills are poor, regardless of the lead quality, your conversion percentage on these leads is going to be very low. You're probably looking at closing in the 2% range in your team's early days. With improved phone skills and better targeted ads, you can see that rise to 3+% over time.

I recommend setting up a $1000/month budget to start. Negotiate with your website and lead-management provider before signing a contract. See if they'll manage your AdWords account for free or at little cost to you.

Facebook Ads

Of all the social media platforms, Facebook is the most ubiquitous among those people who are old enough to buy and sell homes. Facebook ads produce some of the cheapest but lowest converting of all the internet lead sources — and that's OK. I'll say it again; in those first few months of getting your buyer agent team up and running, the quantity of low-cost leads is everything.

One of the first questions to ask when planning a Facebook ad campaign is "Who am I targeting?" Unlike Google AdWords, Facebook's campaign manager has access to enough data on its users that it can target very specific types of prospects. For buyer leads, you're most likely going to be targeting folks between the ages of 25 and 45, although this is not a hard and fast rule. A notable exception would arise if you wanted to target people who are considering a move to a retirement community.

The next consideration is location. Choose those areas where you want your agents to work anyway, and then target the renters in that area. For instance, let's say that you're in my hometown of Austin, Texas, and you want to target first-time buyers. I might choose to advertise in a suburb or nearby city that's popular with first-timers, like Pflugerville. I can create an ad targeting people between the ages of 25 and 35 who already live within three miles of Pflugerville, and who have a household income of $60,000 to $90,000 annually.

You can tighten that up even further by focusing your search on specifically those who Facebook thinks are currently renting. I can make that radius even narrower by using the map tool to draw a one-mile-wide circle around an area with a high concentration of apartment complexes. Start with a campaign of neighborhood-specific ads all around your service area.

First-time buyers can be some of the easiest clients to convert because they don't already have existing relationships with other brokerages. If you catch them while they're still renting, you can leverage the fact that they have a hard date when their lease expires, which provides a lot of predictability in terms of when these deals are likely to pop.

LET'S TAKE A LOOK AT A FEW SAMPLE ADS THAT WORK.

Keep the ad image simple. For geographically targeted ads, use a photo of a landmark in that area, or maybe the entrance sign to the property's subdivision. (Make sure you have the rights to use any images you purchase, and be aware of laws pertaining to the use of photos of one commercial entity to advertise another without permission.) If you have a listing in the neighborhood or can get permission to use a photo of a neighborhood listing, that works well too. For the "Stop Making Your Landlord Rich!" ad, you can use a cheap stock image of an angry businessperson or the like.

Another great call-to-action for Facebook ads is the advertising of free, downloadable white papers with eye-catching titles like "The 7 Mistakes First-Time Home Buyers Make," "5 Questions You Should Ask Your Future Real Estate Agent," or "9 Secret Programs for First-Time Home Buyers." These free reports are easy to create using templates from Microsoft Office Online or Google Docs. You can even subscribe to an information service like Keeping Current Matters for their stock reports, which are easily customizable using PowerPoint or Google Slides. The ads will redirect prospects to very simple landing pages created to convert high percentages of clicks to leads.

The landing page requires the prospect to input his or her email address and/or phone number to download the PDF. The lead's signup information is sent to your inbox. It's that simple.

Our favorite vendor for this service is **Leadpages** (lp.wirbook.com). The system integrates with different database and email marketing programs, many of which are free to use.

Sphere Marketing (That Doesn't Suck)

All of your new lead-generation do-dads are super fun to experiment with, but that doesn't mean you should give up on the most proven business development strategy for residential real estate brokers: marketing to past clients and spheres of influence.

If you mention "building your database" to most agents, you're likely to get objections about how building a list of sphere contacts takes too long and delivers few immediate results. Traditional database marketing can feel a bit uninspired, especially for the younger generation of agents who think monthly pop-bys and recipe postcards are profoundly uncool.

Most agents receive the same stock advice: Harass everyone you know once a week until someone, anyone, cries uncle and gives you a referral.

Whether they begin their careers at big-box brokerage houses or mom-and-pop shops, most agents receive the same stock advice: Harass everyone you know once a week until someone, anyone, cries uncle and gives you a referral. That's a good way to burn your lists and to burn out your new agents. Most of the people with whom you truly want to be in business will find this scorched-earth approach to business development uncomfortable, to say the least.

Would you rather demand referrals until someone relents, or would you prefer to earn them? Sure, it's OK for your agents to call their spheres and let them know all about their new career (or new company, if they're veterans). But what would happen if we came at the rest from a perspective of service instead of scarcity?

Start by giving away your skills and content for free, which will build your credibility and cement your place in the mind of each of your sphere contacts. First, use a search engine like Google to look for a real estate sphere "memory jogger." There are many kinds out there, and they're all reasonably good at getting the job done. A memory jogger is a long list of occupations and other identifiers that you can use to remind you of all the contacts you have. The nice lady at the corner dry cleaners lives in a house. Maybe she rents it and dreams of buying some day, or maybe she owns it and is a future seller. Either way, chances are that she wouldn't mind knowing what homes in that neighborhood are selling for, so ask if she would like to be set up on a once-monthly market snapshot of what's going on in the subdivision. Obtain her email and phone number and add her to your database. Make sure that you set up that market snapshot email to go out automatically so you've made good on your word. Your property search site and lead management should be able to easily handle this type of auto-delivered email.

After the contact is added to your database, you can also set them to receive a monthly email that delivers relevant and specific information about market trends, tips for sellers in your area, etc. (Stay away from nationally syndicated copy-and-paste content; most readers can spot this generalized fluff from a mile away, and they'll opt-out in droves.) Instead, write your own short updates and record YouTube videos where you deliver interesting content. You can embed those in the emails with the help of a tool like BombBomb video email. (Eventually you will want to employ the services of a marketing coach like Vyral Marketing to help you stay super-consistent and relevant in your messaging.) Each year, an average of one out of every twelve people in your database should send you a referral lead if you have done your marketing in a way that is consistent and relevant.

Quarterly phone calls are important to add another dimension to the connection that you're incubating with each prospect.

I hope that at this point you're energized and excited about the ways to build an overflowing pipeline of buyer leads! If you're feeling overwhelmed, don't. Remember that I've paid the tuition for all of these lessons so that you don't have to, and everything I'm presenting to you here is proven to be effective. Now, let's take a look at the ninja tactics you can use to procure listings for your new team.

Part II: Hunting for Sellers

So you've been in a bunker for two weeks setting up lead-generation systems for the buyer agents — great! What's next?

Building your buyer team infrastructure allows you to turn your attention to your other job — being a full-time listing agent. Just like you created those opportunities for the buyer team, you're going to focus now on efficient, inexpensive ways to quickly create an impressive listing inventory.

Leads from Buyer Agents

Considering all the effort you've just spent on creating leads for your buyer team, it's time to focus on the best way for those guys to return the favor! One hard lesson that our team learned over and over was that 20% of the buyer leads your agents speak with do have another home to sell, but you won't know that unless you ask the question. One of your most important training items is going to be to make sure that your buyer agents are including in their scripts something like this:

Just out of curiosity, are you all currently renting in the area or do you own your home? Oh you own your home — fantastic! By the way, are you planning on selling that home so that you can purchase the new property?

I took for granted that all of my early buyer agents were asking this question. After all, it was part of the packet of scripts I threw at them in training!

Then I hired a brand-new agent named Scott. Scott kept forwarding all of these potential seller leads, and we started booking appointments. We closed five listings in a five months because of those leads. I pored over Scott's leads to see where he was getting all of these cherry opportunities and, to my surprise, his leads were just like everyone else's. The difference was simply that Scott was asking the right questions every single time he spoke with a buyer prospect. He understood that more listings for the company equals more organic leads for the buyer agent team.

Train and retrain your buyer agents to ask the question. Don't allow them to take phone shifts or internet leads until they've proven to you that this is part of their standard approach to scripting.

If a new buyer agent finds a listing opportunity, I'd encourage you to let that agent shadow a listing appointment. Tagging along will either help buyer agents determine that they'd eventually like to serve on the listing team, or it will cement a preference to work with buyers only.

Remember that the buyer agent is the only person who has actual rapport with the prospect at this point. The benefit to you as the listing agent is that the buyer specialist is able to lend credibility to you, which can make for a slam-dunk appointment. Some personality types will build a bond quickly with a buyer specialist who prospects on them over the phone. Even if the buyer agent has never met the prospect face to face, having that familiar voice there at the meeting can mean the difference between getting the agreement signed and walking away empty-handed.

Also keep in mind that your buyer agent team is your training ground for new listing agent talent. When it's time for you to step away from listings, it's likely that your listing agent roster will mostly consist of agents who started out with you on the buyer team.`

Your buyer agent team is your training ground for new listing agent talent.

Expired, Withdrawn, and FSBO Calls

These tried and true lead sources can create a mountain of opportunity that most agents will either find exhilarating or exhausting. They are tough leads to book for appointments, and they're often unrealistic on price and not huge fans of agents in general.

Big-box brokers have been teaching brand-new agents to call these leads for decades, so when a listing expires or withdraws, the seller often receives several dozen calls the next day, and those continue for weeks. The lack of experience and skill on the part of these newbie agent callers often causes even more frustration for the prospects.

When you're just entering the business and prospecting on these leads, an already annoyed seller who detects your lack of confidence is more likely to verbally eviscerate you over the phone than to book you for a listing appointment.

For this reason, scripts are everything, and role play is essential. Remember, you must change up your role-play partners if you want to really challenge yourself and prepare for the different personality types you'll encounter over the phone.

Expired/withdrawn/FSBO prospecting also warrants investing a bit of coin into a system that can help ferret out seller contact information. The ideal software solution can also dial those contact numbers in a way that is streamlined yet compliant with applicable regulations. I recommend you check out Vulcan7 (vulcan7.wirbook.com). This system has been a key component of my team's listing operation for years. It seems to produce more accurate seller contact information than competing products, and it's also extremely easy to use. Occasionally the system will connect you with a family member of the person who is selling the home, but with the right scripting those family members are most often happy to help connect you with the homeowner directly.

Obtaining quality phone numbers for withdrawn or expired listings is an ongoing struggle. You may be able to leverage your MLS to provide a permanent record of contact information for those listings. Each one of those failed entries was once an active listing, right? If your MLS hasn't gone the way of the centralized showing service, then there's a high probability that the agent reports for each active listing contain a seller contact number (or two, or a few). So if we periodically download PDF copies of all the active property profiles in MLS, then eventually we have a pretty killer database of listing profile sheets that likely have some good contact info for the sellers. (And because they're PDFs, they're searchable.) Before you implement this tactic, I recommend checking with your local MLS to make sure there are no rules against this type of archive-mining.

At this point, half of your day should be devoted to calling potential listing prospects.

At this point, half of your day should be devoted to calling potential listing prospects. Screen the last three years of expired and withdrawn listings in your MLS and exclude those that were marketed again and subsequently sold. It's likely that many of those listings failed to sell because they didn't have enough equity two years ago, and you can scoop them up now that values are up and loan balances have been paid down.

What Not to Do

There's a lot of buzz right now around sending mailers to expired/withdrawn/FSBO sellers either immediately before or calling them on the phone, after calling them, or both. Some are simple postcards advertising a unique selling proposition, but other programs are much more sophisticated and can include professionally produced DVDs that tell your team's story. These "shock-and-awe" kits are tempting because they look cool and make you feel like a badass, but they're expensive to produce and cumbersome to implement consistently.

Totally forget about direct mail at this stage.

In fact, I want you to totally forget about direct mail at this stage. Rely on the phone. Invest your time in practicing your scripts and objection handlers to increase the quality of your conversations, and then increase the quantity of those dials. When the company revenue is spewing, you can begin leveraging marketing over prospecting. A mixture of both is what we recommend as your team grows.

Other Inexpensive Means of Generating Seller Leads

Once your expired/withdrawn/FSBO prospecting machine is up and running, you can explore some other inexpensive seller lead-generation techniques. One affordable way to meet sellers is through a private service called ZBuyer (zbuyer.wirbook.com). ZBuyer runs national advertising campaigns targeting distressed sellers. They might run a campaign for people who Google terms like "I need a cash offer on my house tomorrow." I'll show you how to build a machine capable of making cash offers yourself in later chapters, but for now, just know that most of the leads procured from these campaigns are not in as dire straits as they imagine. Often they are current on their mortgages but concerned they can't make next month's payment or have recently fallen behind and are actually months away from the first foreclosure notice.

For our Austin team, ZBuyer costs about $125 per month and returns roughly 10 to 15 leads per month. (Check out competing service Fast Home Offer as well.) The leads are not exclusive, which means that you should assume that other agent subscribers are receiving the same leads. There's nothing wrong with a little competition, so make sure that you call the leads first and get an appointment before anyone else gets to them.

Remember those Facebook ads we employed for the buyer team? You can use the same targeting mechanism to go after sellers as well. Create an ad that offers something like "Home values are up. Want to know what your home is worth? Click here to find out!" The conversion rate is only 1%, though. Lots of people want to know what their home is worth but have no motivation to sell.

Door knocking can also be useful here, and it's a great way to build your database of pipeline sellers. But you really have to focus on a few areas and hit them consistently if you're going to stand out as the neighborhood expert. Since the only expense involved in door knocking is shoe leather, it can be a high-return endeavor, but it's so time-intensive that it's difficult to leverage your time well. Plus, door knocking isn't scalable. Use this tactic sparingly, preferably at the end of the quarter when the budget leaves little room to do anything more expensive.

One way to create long-term listing leads is to use a dialer to prospect around neighborhoods. Circle prospecting, as it's called, rarely produces immediate opportunities but is a much more leveraged use of your limited time, since you can have many more conversations per hour on a dialer than you can while door knocking around a neighborhood. The Mojo dialer that I mentioned earlier in this chapter is the preferred tool for this task. It includes a simple map-based feature that allows the user to draw a box around the preferred area to pull a list of landlines in the neighborhood that have been scrubbed against the National Do Not Call Registry. Mojo is the most efficient way to dial these numbers, as it has an option to dial with three lines wide open. It hangs the other two lines up when someone answers. (Again, check the regulations governing use of an auto-dialer in your jurisdiction.)

Here's a script you can use when circle prospecting:

Hi there, my name is Chris Watters. I'm a real estate agent in the area. I'm just calling to conduct a quick survey to see if you have any interest in potentially selling your home in the next 12 months.

Once you've identified them as an opportunity at 6, 9, or 12 months down the road, you can save them in your lead-management system with an automated follow-up plan. You'll ask them for an email address and say "Mr./Ms. Seller, I'd love to send you a market snapshot to keep you up to speed on what's going on in your neighborhood."

Use your property search site's automated search tool to send a monthly email showing active and pending listings in the prospect's neighborhood. A good property search tool will also show you if and when the homeowner opens the email, clicks a link, or forwards the message to a friend.

Here's a note about setting up a market snapshot function: Make sure that the automated search criteria are specific enough to be of interest to the prospect but also broad enough to return 10+ results. This can prove challenging in times of extremely low inventory. Your MLS may also feed recently sold listing data to your property search site in addition to active listings and those pending sale. This feature is not available everywhere, so check with your MLS system administrators.

THE SALES TEAM

By this point, you understand that your escape plan is predicated on your ability to identify and hire key talent. Another "aha" for you right now should be that the quality of your early hires will determine how quickly you can parachute out of the daily transactional grind. Hire the wrong buyer agents in the first year, and you'll have no well of talent to draw from when it comes time to promote someone to the team leader and listing agent roles. Without finding those people, you can forget about ever relinquishing your title of Captain Everything.

Let's go over some basics about recruiting and hiring in the Early Climb and beyond.

The Mechanics of Hiring

In the section on early team technology, I mentioned employing a recruitment platform like HiringThing.com to run ads and begin the candidate screening process. (HiringThing and ZipRecruiter can also broadcast ads to Indeed.com and Craigslist, which will be a huge timesaver for you.) Let's go over some of the basic elements of the hiring process before we talk about how to find those candidates.

Screening Tools and Interview Questions

Once you've got a few folks interested in working for you, what do you do with them? Applicants enter the funnel via the hiring platform, and then it's time for you to whittle that list down to a manageable number of promising candidates to interview over the phone.

The first screening tool I recommend is a DISC personality assessment. In your early days, you can direct people to free resources to obtain their own reports. (For example, Tony Robbins has a great DISC assessment tool that's free on his website.) I'm reasonably certain that you've already been indoctrinated in the ways of the DISC assessment, given its ubiquity in the real estate industry. Just in case, here is the concept of the DISC assessment in a nutshell. The tool uses four terms[2] to describe a person's behavioral traits:

Dominant

Influential

Steady

Conscientious

We won't dive deeply into the intricacies of the test here, but suffice it to say that most of us lead with one major indicator and have varying degrees of the other characteristics, which also define our behavior. When someone reads your DISC assessment, they'll usually describe you using the two most prominent characteristics, like ID or SC. Traditionally, people who are Dominant and Influential are steered toward sales for their abilities to persuade and engage, while those who align with Steadiness and Conscientiousness shine in support roles.

I've learned to use the DISC assessment as a tool, but not necessarily a

[2]Some versions of the profile use the terms *dominance, inducement, submission,* and *compliance.*

disqualifier. If the applicant has an SC personality and a proven track record of success in computer programming but hasn't closed a sale in six months at Broker X, then the DISC test offers just a confirmation that no, this one's not right for the listing agent role. Consider the assessment a data point, and make decisions based on the candidate as a whole.

Look Deep Before You Leap

Don't assume that everyone who applies actually has the chops to get the job done. Read each resume with a critical eye. Do they have the work experience, education, and licensing cred to match the requirements laid out in the ad? It may sound obvious, but many applicants don't read the ad at all and just apply for every job in the category. It's easy to get excited about the first applications and book your interviews only to find out later that the candidate was never a match for the position.

After you've reviewed the work history and DISC assessment, invite likely candidates to a phone interview. Phone appointments are not the time to put applicant on the hot seat; rather, they're opportunities to build rapport with candidates and get a feel for who they are.

Ask Jane Candidate to tell you about herself, what her short- and long-term goals are, and what kind of role she's in now. How does she like that role, and what would make her think about leaving it at this time? What does she enjoy doing outside of work? (Keep in mind that some topics should be avoided; for example, steer clear of questions about familial status, age, or religious affiliation, at least when interviewing W-2 employees.) This is a very preliminary discussion; see how well she builds rapport with people and how well she can communicate with someone over the phone, since that's such a huge predictor of success in our industry.

Core Values and Personal Story

If Jane's phone skills are up to par and she builds rapport well, bring her into the office for an interview. For the in-person interview, you'll perform a few different assessments, including a custom interview questionnaire. (Go to bonus.wirbook.com to download the PDF.) The questionnaire dives deeper into questions about how candidates view themselves.

There are so many eye-opening answers that come from that first questionnaire. "What is the one thing that you get complimented on the most?" can be telling, since the answer that many candidates tend to give is actually more along the lines of "what I've been complimented on that means a lot to me." The candidate that answers with "my eyes" may be in a different place than the candidate who answers with "my authentic personality."

Another favorite is "If there's one characteristic or quality that you could have more of instantly, what would it be?" Some people might say "organizational skills" or "discipline." We're still playing with kid gloves on during this stage, so don't penalize candidates for being honest, but do use answers as jumping off points for more discussion.

The next thing we'll dial into is a **core values questionnaire** (also available at bonus.wirbook.com). One of my favorite questions is "If you were teaching a class to college students on the core values they should hold onto throughout their lives, which values would you emphasize?" The questionnaire is going to help Joe Candidate drill down to what his core values really are. He may be 30 years old and may have never considered the question of what drives him in life. The results can be eye-opening for the interviewee.

The key thing I want to spot early is a misalignment between the core values of the person and the values of my organization.

What are the red flags I'm looking for with this tool? The key thing I want to spot early is a misalignment between the core values of the person and the values of my organization. If Joe lists as core values "tranquility, consistency, and balance," then pause to consider how likely he will be to enjoy the breakneck pace, crazy work hours, and organized chaos of your rapidly expanding business.

Frankly, core values are simply more important than previous

experience. You can train any reasonably intelligent individual to be a great agent—as long as he or she shares your values. Companies like Google, Zappos, and Apple created their successes by prioritizing core values when building their teams. The people who are the right fit for your organization will buy into your vision. You'll build a pervasive feeling that they're working on something much greater than their own personal goals (or those of the founders).

The third and final document that I go over with the candidate is the **personal story interview**. This is exactly what it sounds like, a great big expanse in which interviewees describe their professional lives in terms of dates and occupations, all the way back to high school: What did you do in each period, for how long, and what were you paid? What did you learn and where were the problems?

This interview is very common in our industry, and for good reason. The personal story interview is incredibly revealing, since you will routinely have candidates who tell you about short-lived occupations or disastrous business ventures that they failed to mention on their resumes.

Residential real estate sales is a fallback, "I'll give it a shot" option for people who fail out of other industries. Real estate agency work has a broad appeal to people because they've "always loved looking at houses." Many prospective agents whom I've interviewed seem to believe that our job is mostly about carrying a clipboard and pointing at crown moulding for a living. Even worse are the people who enter the business because the hours are flexible. These people will not mesh with your structured team and high expectations. You've got to screen out folks who aren't really looking to do the hard things required to succeed at a top-performer level.

On the questionnaire, the first thing I look for is an upward trajectory. Temporary setbacks happen, but a candidate's general progression should indicate previous success and a tendency to move up in title and income with each job change.

Then I compare the core values assessment with the personal story results, because these two assessments are really just the opposite sides of the same coin. Here's an example of what I mean. On my company's big sign that says "FREEDOM," mentioned earlier in this chapter, each of the letters stands for one of our core values. *F* is for "Fiercely Committed." A candidate's life story may show a previous position that lasted three months. Candidate Jane tells me that she quit that job because it was challenging and she basically just gave up. Regardless of her stated core values, her life story tells me that she hasn't practiced commitment in her professional life as of late.

The Practical Interview

Once the applicants have completed the in-depth first interview, you'll decide, based on the results, whether you want to push them forward to a second interview. The next interview is a practical interview. Don't tell the applicant that it's a practical interview; just tell them you have one more interview for them to get through and to allocate about an hour and a half. The position the candidate is applying for will determine the nature of the tasks assigned.

For example, if you're hiring an executive assistant, you would set up a series of challenges that this person has to complete in 60 minutes. The last time I hired an executive assistant, I told all the candidates that I wanted them to find front-row tickets to a sold-out concert and set a challenging budget for those seats.

I also want to test their math skills, so I gave them a complicated and very real-world example of calculating buyer agent and listing agent commission checks for the month. I used a graduated commission split model as an example, with the first two deals paid out at 40% of gross, the second two at 45% and the fifth deal at 50%. I asked for the net to the company and the net to the agent.

The third exercise is to gauge their ability to communicate and coordinate with outside vendors. In the past I've asked executive assistant candidates to create a list of the top three area bookkeepers they would recommend that we work with and to explain why. There's an element of judgment to this task, of course. I want to see that they've used critical thinking skills to determine which vendors should be at the top of the list.

Keep in mind that all of this has to be completed within 60 minutes. This practical application of how the candidates approach tasks is the absolute best predictor of their future behavior under stress! All support staff should be able to problem-solve, so I recommend that you tailor your interviews to look for a solid foundation in mathematics. Math skills are a huge predictor of a person's general problem-solving skills. We create similarly relevant interview tasks for other support roles, like closing coordinator and listing manager, as well as for sales positions.

> *You will rue the day that you hire an agent or staffer who cannot use a computer.*

A key to any practical interview is the technology piece. Your practical interview should have your applicants using basic office software and the web, plus any skills that are specific to the role (to a degree that is reasonable to expect of a candidate prior to being trained).

I once hired an applicant whose resume was sterling. She supposedly knew every inch of Microsoft Office and the Google suite of products. I did not put her through a practical interview. When she showed up for her first day of work, she spent *half an hour* trying to figure out how to attach a file to an email message in Gmail. It gets better. Someone finally noticed her struggling and showed her how to do it. An hour later when it came time to repeat the task, she'd completely forgotten how to attach the file.

I was baffled. I spent a month trying to make it work with her, only to have to let her go. By that time, she had cost me a month's worth of headaches and wasted time, plus several pissed-off clients and a few thousand dollars in compensation.

I can't emphasize this point enough. You will rue the day that you hire an agent or staffer who cannot use a computer. There is no employee, no matter how likeable, talented, or full of potential, who can overcome this deficiency. Don't do it.

As we'll see in a few pages, your immediate need in the Early Climb is for buyer agents. For their practical interviews you could give them 15 minutes' worth of basic script training and a list of 50 numbers — and then put them on the phone already! Take note of whether they hesitate before dialing, become flustered, or get distracted easily. Do they get more comfortable and confident with each call? Do they sound like they are at all enjoying themselves? Does the candidate naturally approach sales from a consultative place? Do they dig deep and ask a lot of questions, or do you hear them getting defensive? Great salespeople are always consultative; steer clear of emotional candidates who are triggered easily.

Interviews Are Over! What's Next?

I'm going to recommend that you hire no one who doesn't pass every portion of the interview. It's painful to take a pass on someone who is friendly and relatable, especially in those times where you need help badly (such as the Early Climb). But in this case, "doubt means don't."

Ask yourself a couple of key questions. "Is this someone I would spend time with outside of work?" "Is this someone I really want representing me and my brand?" Going into business with the wrong individual is profoundly costly from a financial perspective and can have even more adverse effects on your stress level. It truly does take only one bad apple to destroy your reputation, and chances are that the warning signs were apparent—but discounted—in the first round of interviews.

If Joe Candidate clears all of the interviews above with flying colors, bring him in for a 30-minute follow-up meeting and, if all goes well, make him an offer.

Who to Hire First

In the Early Climb, the prescription for recruitment is simple; you need buyer agents, and you need them now. Keep in mind that what you have to show them at this point may feel a little skinny. Your marketing machine is still revving up, so right now you've got your initial listing inventory and a few buyer lead sources that are beginning to produce.

Don't let your lean operation pollute your own thinking with limiting beliefs about not being able to attract the right people early on. The residential real estate industry in your town is starved for exactly

> Agents want one-on-one training and support, and they want leads. You can guarantee both.

what you're offering. You will find that many agents are not excited about getting lost in the shuffle at a corporate mega-brokerage. They want one-on-one training and support, and they want leads. You can guarantee both, so you're actually at an advantage — but you have to buy into that and **know the value of what you're offering.**

The Best Buyer Agent to Hire (and the One to Avoid!)

My FAVORITE buyer specialists to hire are agents in their first or second year in the business but who are struggling to close deals at big-box outfits. Let's look at Buyer Agent Taylor. Some agent-recruiter hybrid told her she'd be amazing in real estate, signed her up with the mothership and then promptly vanished. This newbie has paid an initial training fee and even purchased some of the broker's very expensive training "upgrades," even though she's living off of credit cards to make this new career work.

Taylor's working from home, desperately stalking her sphere for referrals and burning her own list in the process. She's clawed her way to closing a handful of deals in the first year but is getting desperate, living on leasing leads and other scraps left behind by her "mentors." Still, she's hell-bent on making this career work.

Why is this person my ideal candidate? First, the bumpy launch at the mega-broker provides the context to know that a team like yours is the equivalent of real estate Candyland. Your first office could be the size of a Prius and Taylor would still be excited to have a tiny desk and a few buyer leads to call her own. The appreciation is there, and that's the key.

It's important that she's done a few deals on her own. If she hung in for a year at the big-box, she should've been able to close four or more transactions through her own brute-force efforts, plus some leases. (If she hasn't closed anything at all, I'd take a pass on the basis that she's probably not resourceful.)

She's also not ready to quit even if I don't hire her, which is important. Never hire someone who tells you that they're probably about to leave real estate for another career. An interviewee with one foot out the industry door is already working on plans B and C. You will almost certainly not be able to re-energize such employees about straight commission agency work at that point.

For now, you simply don't have time to teach someone what "escrow" means or how to use a Supra key.

If you can, also stay away from brand-new agents fresh out of real estate school in this crucial period. Yes, you will miss out on some talent, but as Captain Everything, there's only one of you, and you have a ton of other stuff to worry about in addition to your new buyer agent team. Later in your development, when you've fleshed out your organization to include leaders dedicated to developing talent, you can relax this rule for the right candidate. For now, you simply don't have time to teach someone what *escrow* means or how to use a Supra key.

More importantly, brand-new agents don't have the context that our ideal candidate has. They lack the experience that tells them that what you are offering is special and is the environment that's the most likely to create a quick career launch. The lack of context breeds a lack of appreciation. Brand-new agents will take for granted that the mountain of resources you're providing is the norm, and within a year, they'll get cocky and want to try their hand at a brokerage with a higher commission split and a slick recruitment team.

On the other hand, you shouldn't hire very experienced agents either. Agents who have been in the business for more than two years have likely developed poor habits when it comes to prospecting, coming into the office, and calling leads. They've been working from home for long enough that it's spoiled them; they are unlikely to be rehabilitated into professionals who show up at 8 a.m. of their own volition, ready to prospect for hours on end.

Finally, don't hire a candidate who is not enthusiastic about the terms of your independent contractor relationship. Maybe Joe Candidate is self-aware enough to know that he needs the leads and will make more money with you, but if you get the sense that the splits or prospecting expectations have him holding his nose to make this relationship work, you need to cut bait. He will always be looking for another, bigger and better deal.

Now Go Find Your Team

Let's go back to where we are in the Early Climb stage. Right now, hiring is very simple; this is the time when you're going to use laser-like focus to build your first big money-maker and the training ground for future leaders: your buyer specialist team.

Take a moment to ask why you're going to separate your sales department into a listing team and a buyer team. The short answer is that specializing in one side of the business allows a salesperson to get ninja good at a short list of tasks by performing them over and over again. Limiting new agents' responsibilities helps you focus them on the short list of tasks that are crucial to creating success.

It's a hard and fast rule in our model that every agent starts off on the buyer team. Why is that? There are several reasons, but they all stem from the same reality. Home buying is a "want" item and home selling is a "need" item. So buyers are slow, deliberate, and generally very forgiving of rookie mistakes. Sellers are impatient and stressed, and they need concrete answers right now. The wide variety in transactional experiences that agents have while servicing buyers is what prepares them for sellers' very specific needs and rapid-fire questions.

Most buyers will enter your environment through a casual inquiry like a sign call or website registration. Build a little rapport and you can persuade some of them to work with you.

Sellers are likely interviewing three or four agents, so if an agent doesn't walk out of a listing appointment with a signed agreement, the chances of snagging the listing are quite low. Nail the audition, or you don't get the gig. Also, seller leads are generally more expensive to create than buyer leads. All of this adds up to mean that only an experienced agent with high conversion skills should be in the listing agent role.

For every one or two buyer agents who work out, you'll probably have hired two or three who didn't. But those one or two successful buyer specialists will grow with your team. Agent Taylor will practice with you for about a year, and after 25 transactions, cross-train for listings if she wants more. (We'll talk about other ways that her career can unfold in the next chapter.) I can't stress this enough — don't lose sight of the fact that your first listing agent or team leader is very likely to be in your first cohort of buyer specialists.

Prospecting for Buyer Agents

The key to creating good response is writing a killer ad, and a killer ad starts with a catchy headline. You need a hook. "New Firm Seeks Agent" won't cut it anymore. Try something that grabs attention, like:

Make $100K in Your First Year — Or I'll Make up the Difference! *

It's true; you really can make this offer to the agent community, even though your team is in bootstrap mode. In the body of the ad, say that some terms and conditions apply to this guarantee. When agent candidates inquire about this guarantee (and who wouldn't?), get them in for an interview and, at the end, go over the terms of the guarantee. Those terms should lay out minimum prospecting goals for the year, including >50 open houses, >1000 new sphere database contacts added, and >60 unique phone contacts made each week. For a real go-getter, one open house per week (with two built-in weeks off) and three database contacts added per day is not unreasonable. A plucky agent candidate who energetically pursues those goals should hit $100k or close to it. (If agents make only $95k after all that effort, I'll happily write them a check for the $5k difference, with the knowledge that year two will be amazing.)

You can send email asks out as well, but response is generally pretty low. A sample recruitment email might have a simple subject line like "I have a buyer referral." The body of the email should look like a true personal email; no flashy graphics, just text:

Hey guys, I've got an opportunity. It's a buyer looking for a home in Cedar Park. To be quite honest, I've got more leads than I can handle, and I'm looking for more agents in the Austin area. It's okay if you're newer in the business; if you've been in the business between three months and two years, I'd really like to send you some of the these leads.

Ads and emails are great, but where you're going to have the most success in prospecting for buyer agents is on the phone. The agents I recommend that you target have been in the business for 3 to 24 months. I'm less concerned about finding someone who has produced at a high level and more apt to hire someone who's got what it takes but hasn't been given the opportunity. The candidate has to be ready to dive in full-time; hiring someone who waits tables at night or has another job will generally not work out. There needs to be an upward trajectory in their life story and values congruent with our own, but a proven track record of 20 closings is not required.

> When recruiting agents, leads are your currency.

Keep in mind that when recruiting agents, leads are your currency. If you have the business to share, just about any agent is going to be willing to meet with you — especially someone who is newer to the business. It doesn't take long for new agents to figure out that just because they have a real estate license, people don't just automatically line up for help with their real estate needs. Leads get them in the door, and your team culture, training, and support keep them sticking around.

Don't be afraid to go to your competitors' company rosters and just start calling. The script goes something like this:

Hey there, my name is Chris Watters with Watters International Realty. I was reading your profile online, and it seems to me that you're a hungry, ambitious agent who is looking for more. I'm actually in a very unique position; I have a great opportunity that I want to share with you. The fact is that I've got more leads than I can handle, and if I don't get some help with them, things are going to start falling through the cracks. I've love to sit down with you and see if maybe I can direct some of these your way and see how it goes. If it's a good relationship, maybe we can partner together. Got a quick few minutes to sit down with me for coffee this week?

If they don't answer, here's a voicemail script you can leave for them:

Hey, I've got this opportunity for you.
Give me a call when you get a chance.

Yep, it's that simple. Tack anything more onto the voicemail script and you won't receive a call back. It doesn't work to leave a message about wanting to send them leads or recruit them onto your team. You won't get a response, and you're just teaching them what phone number not to answer. You just want them to call you back so that you can have a discussion and see if it's someone you might want to meet.

The goal is to set 10 appointments per week with potential recruits. Make the calls, leave the voicemails, but know ahead of time that agents are frequently not going to return phone calls and will sometimes even flake on appointments. That's just part of the deal. It's not you!

You're going to have to use the same persistence as when you prospect on buyer and seller leads. You're going to need to spend a minimum of one to two hours every day prospecting agents to join your company. That's 5 to 10 hours per week to get to your 10 appointment goal. That's a high number, I know, especially when you're going on listing appointments and running other areas of your business. This is a nonstop thing, and you're putting in a lot of hours.

On the phone and at the first in-person meeting, make sure you assure the agents of confidentiality, since there's a good chance that they'll decide stay put with their current broker when it's all said and done. You don't want to do anything to jeopardize that relationship if an agent's not a fit for your team. Begin the interview with the rapport-building questions, finding commonalities between yourself and the prospect on areas like how each of you chose to practice real estate, what you like to do for fun outside work, etc.

Once the ice is broken and the candidate opens up a bit, turn to the next line of questioning. Ask what Joe Candidate's challenges are. For 99% of agents who have been in the business under two years, the greatest challenge is going to be business development, i.e., not enough leads. They don't know what tools to use to generate leads or even what scripts to use if they were handed a random lead today. They're paralyzed by the lack of direction and spend hours alone in their home offices wondering what to do next.

Ask the candidate questions that will lead him to think about those pain points. You're in a unique position to solve those problems for the agents, since you have leads coming in and can teach new recruits how to convert them. You have the technology tools and everything else that they need to be successful. All they have to do is implement the systems and follow your lead to success. If you encounter a candidate who thinks you are blowing smoke about having leads, bust out your laptop and show them the lead-management tool and all of the folks that are pinging your website.

After the formal interview process, how do you ask a buyer agent to go steady?

Frank, you know what? I really enjoy talking with you, and I think we get along great. I can imagine you doing a really great job in front of buyers and sellers, and it sounds like one of your biggest needs is leads, which I have plenty of. I'd love to extend an invitation for you to join our company. What do you say? We could rock and roll tomorrow if you're ready.

The next question from candidates inevitably is "That all sounds great — but what's the split?"

This can be a really telling moment. Many average agents have tunnel vision about commission splits. Keep in mind that struggling candidates are probably also weighing the benefits of working with a low-fee brokerage that offers no leads and light support.

The splits you offer to buyer agents are up to you, but don't publish them without running numbers based on the agents' expected production levels and the average price point in your market. Read this book in its entirety and think about the future of your team. Where will your leads come from, and how much will they cost? What other fixed expenses will you have, and do those become more or less expensive per agent as the team grows into Version 2.0 and beyond? Think about the combinations of commission percentages and additional fees you can charge that stay consistently profitable as you grow AND still allow you to establish the clear-cut value required to recruit and retain buyer agents.

Show them the bigger picture. Share with them that you're building a team of coordinators to help with service delivery so that they can go out there and focus on the dollar-productive activities of prospecting and meeting buyers. Tell them about how you'll help them triple their production through company-generated leads and killer sales training.

You'll sit across from them and explain their current splits of X% aren't that awesome if the broker isn't helping them build their businesses. But sometimes they're just too attached to that percentage; there's no reasoning with them. They may have been sold a bill of goods in the past by a fast-talking big-box team leader, and your pitch may sound too good to be true. After all, your team is built around a concept long-considered heretical in the real estate industry: investing your time and cash into making agents successful.

Here's how you handle the objection from an agent who currently has a more favorable split:

I definitely hear you about the split but let me ask you this. How much do you net now? What are all of your expenses? When you actually look at what your gross income is and you deduct all your expenses, how much are you actually netting?

Listen for expenses that the agent wouldn't pay out of pocket in your model. Remind candidates of the price tag of the systems that you'll provide. (We'll talk more about what you provide in the section on Back Office.) Help candidates connect the dots when it comes to the way you are taking the financial risk off of their shoulders and putting it on your own.

THANKS, BUT NO THANKS

You can send a rejection letter to everyone who applies or reserve that only for the folks whom you've interviewed in person or over the phone. The best practice is to create a template email to let 'em down easy:

Dear <CandidateFirstName>,

Thank you very much for applying for the <PositionName> opportunity. We take hiring very seriously and believe in our responsibility to match you with a position that aligns fully with your skills and natural talents. Unfortunately, we do not have a position available that we believe will be an ideal fit for you at this time. We will keep your application on file in case another opportunity comes available. Thank you again, and best of luck.

If you find yourself in an interview and determine that you are not sitting across from someone who can do the job or represent your company well, don't be afraid to cut the meeting short. Your time is precious and so is the candidate's. It's no fun for the candidate to be cut off mid-interview when things aren't igniting, but it sure beats giving Jane Candidate false hope or wondering if she's going to pass on another opportunity because she thinks she has a chance with your team. Naturally indirect communicators will have trouble with this approach, so remember — stringing the candidate along is unkind; dodging phone calls for the next two weeks is not in alignment with your desire to help others succeed.

COACHING & TRAINING

In this pillar of the Early Climb, we are focused on creating a quick launch for those buyer agents you've recruited. You have serious demands on your time at this stage, which means that your buyer agents have to become self-sufficient and productive on an expedited schedule.

You will accomplish this by creating a 30-day onboarding process. For four hours each day, your buyer agents will spend their time learning the basics of conversion, the foundational DNA of your company, and phone prospecting, all in a group setting. In the first 30 days you'll drive home the concept of core values and what they mean in daily practice. You'll indoctrinate the agents in your mission, vision, and team goals. The agents will also be creating goals of their own while getting used to a level of accountability that is probably new to them. You'll set up their Google environment and get them started on the lead management and call-capture systems.

Because the training process is so time-intensive, do everything you can to avoid training just one person at a time. Group them into cohorts of at least two. Remember that with buyer agents, you should hire four in the hope that one or two will work out.

> *Do everything you can to avoid training just one person at a time.*

Once the new recruits are adept at the technology tools and acquainted with your core values, mission, and vision, you'll really start digging deeper into how to become great salespeople. The first skill you want to help them improve is their mastery of telephone prospecting. If you're planning to create this training program totally on your own, I suggest developing training materials as you go along. That way, when you hire the next class of buyer agents, you don't have to reinvent the wheel with each cohort. At this stage, focus on creating handouts for topics like phone greetings, objection handling, how to build rapport with clients, and how to give a buyer presentation. You'll be teaching all the agents yourself in the beginning, but as you grow we'll talk about how to automate some of the training process. (If all of this sounds daunting, don't stop reading — I'll talk about a way to jumpstart this process a little later, when we talk about your Great Escape.)

The First 30 Days

Here's a breakdown of how your 30-day onboarding process should look. I'll go over the first week in full detail and summarize the following weeks, since you will be training fewer hours starting in the second week so the agents can spend more time calling prospects. Always start your trainees off on a Monday and never in a short holiday week.

Week 1

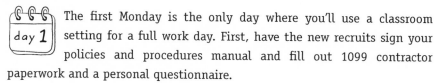 The first Monday is the only day where you'll use a classroom setting for a full work day. First, have the new recruits sign your policies and procedures manual and fill out 1099 contractor paperwork and a personal questionnaire.

The personal questionnaire should feature questions about Agent Taylor's previous work experience, what her goals are, and how she interacts on a team. She and Agent Joe will read their answers aloud to one another and discuss their responses. It's a way of helping the agents bond with one another from the start, which is way more important than it sounds. Creating a cohort of a few people who've been together since Day One provides the agents with support and a sense of comradery from the jump.

Also, you'll present your core values, mission, and vision, as well as handle the transfer of their sales license to your team and any change of sponsorship forms required by your board of Realtors®.

The remainder of Day One is consumed by teaching tech tools like the property search site and lead-management system, Gmail/GCal/GDrive, and your group texting application. (Do not teach your call-capture system yet; your agents are not ready for inbound calls and must prove they're ready for those hot phone leads.) Set them up on the printers and, if necessary, teach them how to scan docs.

 Introduce your sales training methodology. Emphasize the importance of having meaningful, authentic conversations with people and explain how the right scripts help accomplish this goal. Throw in a motivational video about building rapport. (Tony Robbins has a great one about mirroring and tonality on YouTube.) Teach scripting basics, focusing on the tried-and-true "LPMAMA" scripting[3], and walk the agents through their first role plays. Educate the agents on the DISC profile and how we apply those concepts in our phone prospecting.

Prepare the agents for the type of calls they're going to begin making the following day. Circle prospecting numbers are the lowest-stakes leads because they're the coolest. Agents may not be excited about calling cold leads but you can't afford to have them unleashing their novice scripting skills on your coveted inbound leads.

 Direct the agents to circle prospect around neighborhoods using the speed dialers. Prospecting should be preceded by 30 minutes of role play to warm up. Focus on nailing the greeting and developing rapport. Each agent will need an individual speed dialer license if the team will all be prospecting at the same time. Teach the recruits about overcoming phone objections and how to go for the appointment.

---

[3]Location: Where does the buyer want to live?
Price: What is the buyer's price range?
Motivation: How motivated is the buyer?
Approved: Has the buyer been approved for a loan?
Mortgage: What mortgage amount has the buyer been approved for?
Agent: Does the buyer have an agent already?

📅 **day 4** 30 minutes of role-play warm up, then focus on circle prospecting. Book an individual meeting with each agent for the following day (Friday). Set the expectation that you will be reviewing Agent Taylor's progress and discussing whether the program is a fit for her. Teach advanced open house techniques and how to convert lease leads into buyers. Introduce the agents to your vendor partners like the lender (see the Brand Ambassador section for more) and position each vendor as a resource and a go-to for any questions regarding their industry. It's important for each vendor to meet every agent in person. We'll go into that later.

📅 **day 5** Friday is the week one evaluation. Have a frank conversation with the recruit about how this match is working so far. If your gut says to cut the agent from the team, do it now. If you are aggressive about cutting underperformers early, you will occasionally make the wrong call and cut real talent — BUT for every one of those missed opportunities, you'll cut five or 10 folks who would've never produced at a high level. The time and frustration saved are worth the cost of losing a potentially talented agent every now and again.

For the recruits who make this first cut, sit down with them to introduce your goal-setting tool. Walk the agents through the tool, leaving it with them to complete and turn in to you the following Tuesday.

How to screw this up

When I hired my first team leader, he formalized the agent training program and put the first cohort through all-day classroom courses for two weeks. We were trying to download all of our real estate knowledge into their brains. By 11 a.m. they were yawning and checked out, and they retained almost none of what we taught. We learned pretty quickly that it's pointless to teach new agents how to solve appraisal problems when they've never even shown a home before. Excited recruits may want to dive into the mechanics of negotiating contracts. Don't do it; keep them focused on building a pipeline of business. You can teach them how to deliver great service once they have clients to practice on. The earlier they execute deals, the higher your chance of retaining them will be.

Goal Setting

Working with the recruits to set sales goals is crucial, and it's imperative to establish those targets in the agents' first week on the job. As the broker, you can't set these goals for them. If the agents don't come up with these goals themselves, they won't own them. I recommend that you challenge agents to think of their goals in terms of three different numbers.

GOAL SETTING: GETTING NITTY GRITTY

- **First, establish a baseline.** What's the minimum gross income Agent Taylor could accept for the next 12 months? If she makes a dollar less than this figure, she'd consider her effort a failure and probably leave the real estate industry (or move to another brokerage).

- **Ask the agent to make a realistic assessment of her commitment** to showing up and playing all-in, as well as her weaknesses, strengths, and outside factors that are likely to distract her from production. Based on that pragmatic view of herself and her knowledge of the tools you're bringing to bear on her behalf, what does she think she's most likely to produce in the next 12 months?

- **Finally, she needs a stretch goal.** A good rule of thumb when calculating a stretch goal is to have the agent set one that she believes she has a 50% chance of hitting. Anything more, and she's not really stretching; anything less, and she's likely to abandon this goal early because it feels unattainable.

The goal-setting document should take the 12-month income goal and break that down month by month. Have the agents calculate the number of deals it will take them to reach their monthly income goals, and then help them think through the number of appointments, buyer reps, and phone calls it will take to get to that number of closed transactions. The agents may feel daunted by the level of detail, but the juice here is in the process of breaking these goals down into measurable, actionable steps!

The second week is about maximizing phone prospecting time. The objective is to immerse the recruits in their scripts and dialogues until they are memorized. You are looking for a few things here. First, be on the lookout for creative avoidance of the phone. In the first week, everything they are learning is new and exciting. Even phone-averse agents can comply with your instructions when the task is a novelty; in week two, look for agents who achieve abnormally low dial numbers, or who seem to find any excuse not to make the next call. Call reluctance is the number-one problem to root out in your early training; do not accept the agents' excuses about why they're not calling. Bust them as soon as you see it happening.

On Tuesday you'll review the goal-setting document. The big push this week from a training perspective will be about teaching the basics of a buyer presentation, then role playing the presentation for the agents yourself. The expectation is that they will turn around and present a competent buyer presentation to you on Friday. To get ready, they should be presenting to one another first.

 As the team leader, this is an intense training week for you. Teaching contracts and compliance is something that you will farm out very quickly after you move out of Early Climb, but for now, there is no short-cutting the task of making sure that your sales agents are well versed in the transactional process and compliance topics required by your state. An agent who has closed six deals at Broker X, may still not have a good grasp of the contracts, the role of the lender and title company, or how to advise clients on repairs. If Broker X was a big-box shop that relies on "peer support" for ongoing contract questions, expect that their former agents will come to your team with plenty of misconceptions about a variety of topics.

 In week four you are testing the agents on their contractual skills and fine-tuning their buyer presentations, but most importantly you are working on their skills handling their first warm leads. You will be passing off some of your shiny new internet leads for the agents to call, and you'll also be training them on how to handle the all-important inbound phone calls. This may seem like a piece of cake, but for a new agent to master the art of these 30-second auditions takes some time.

Ongoing Activities

Just because your agent clears the initial 30 days of training doesn't mean that they are loosed upon the world without further guidance. Yes, it's true that you are hamstrung in what you can require of buyer agents when it comes to their schedules, etc., but you will hold morning prospecting blocks, and the agents who are long-term fits will happily come to those 8 a.m. to 11 a.m. sessions of their own volition. Agents who are true matches for your organization are self-motivating and enjoy the energy and healthy competition of the office. The same goes for meetings; you probably can't require the agents to be there if they're 1099 contractors, and also, the good ones will show up.

Why do we meet in the mornings for the prospecting sessions? Aren't evenings the preferred times to call? The answer is that yes, the phone answer rate is highest in the early evening. But no, evenings are not our preferred time to call. Let me explain.

When an agent first joins a team like yours, where there's a machine already in place for creating and converting leads, it's easy for them to become overwhelmed. They will probably book appointments earlier than they anticipated, and they still have so much to learn while they service these new prospects. A week goes by, and more new leads come through, but the agents are scrambling to stay on top of the to-do items for the leads from last week, and the week before. Now Lead A wants to see property in the afternoon. Lead B wants to write an offer! How do I get all of this done without working until midnight?

I call these "champagne problems." There's only one solution to avoiding this chaotic, inefficient reactivity. The solution is time-blocking the agent's prospecting so that it gets done and out of the way before distractions arise. That is only consistently possible if it's done in the morning. Remember that the good plan that you implement is far better than the perfect plan that you just can't seem to get around to executing. Prospecting as a team in the morning gets the calls and follow-ups out of the way so that the agent can feel caught up before the property showings, buyer appointments, etc.

Open up your morning prospecting sessions with a 15-minute huddle. Have everyone state a goal for the morning and then have everyone do a quick role play. Insert mini training "bites" as needed, but keep it all under 15 minutes. Jumping on the phone is the priority.

You'll also be hosting a weekly buyer agent team meeting on a day and time that does not conflict with your prospecting blocks. Present a training topic, talk about each agent's wins and losses for the week, and set goals for the week ahead. (Write down these goals yourself and enter them on the agents' calendars for the following week. What good does setting goals do if there is no accountability?)

Monthly, you'll meet with each agent individually to go over their goal-setting document. How are they progressing toward their monthly income goals? If Agent Joe is off track, check out his call, appointment, and buyer rep numbers to isolate where the problem lies. It's helpful to keep a record of the non-income goals as well. What are the items that your agent wants to accomplish outside of pure numbers? Do they want to lose weight or save up for a vacation? Find out what personal goals he's pursuing, and what long-term career milestones you can help him achieve. This will strengthen the bond between you and the agent. If your team knows your main motivator is to help them be successful in all areas of life, you can inspire the kind of loyalty that keeps morale high and turnover low.

Teaching Lead Conversion Basics

Creating great phone habits among your buyer agent team can be a struggle for a rainmaker in the Early Climb stage. But a little concerted effort up front can save you a ton of headaches (and money) down the road.

There are two important aspects to converting leads. The first is your follow-up system and the second is the arsenal of scripts and objection handlers that your agents use to increase conversion rate.

The follow-up system is simply the tools you have at your disposal to engage with the prospect, coupled with plans for touching each lead at regular, planned intervals. The plans need to be simple and repeatable, with a call frequency that is appropriate for different stages of the home-buying process. For example, leads in the "Hot" category are looking to purchase in the next 30 to 90 days, so they should be contacted once per week. Leads in the "Watch" category might be a year out, so an intense plan of weekly phone calls will just alienate them. Whatever your strategy for contacting leads, the most important ingredient is that the rainmaker ensures it gets implemented every time.

The most important pieces are the phone calls, but you should also use text messaging and drip email campaigns to touch the lead in other ways in case they're super phone-averse. Let's use a buyer lead as an example. Let's say that it's a buyer who has registered on your property search site to view one property in your service area. The contact cadence would be as follows:

CONVERTING LEADS

- Call within 15 minutes of registry, using the double-tap method (i.e., call once, don't leave a voicemail, and then call right back so the prospect knows it's an important call).

- Leave a voicemail, followed by a text that says "Is your voicemail working?"

- Start the prospect on an email drip campaign with the first email containing "Is your voicemail working?" in the subject line and nothing in the body.

- Call once per day for the next three days (not leaving voicemails).

- Call again at 7 days, then 14, 21, and 30 days.

- Still no response? Transfer to an inactive (archive) status in your lead-management system, and continue with email drip campaign. Go to bonus.wirbook.com to download our most successful drip email campaigns.

The juice here is in the implementation and the consistency with which you oversee your agents' use of these tools and techniques. Pig-headed discipline in telephone prospecting is not what most agents consider a great time. Yet lackadaisical enforcement from you as the rainmaker can be catastrophic, as the agents will creatively avoid performing this task, which is admittedly uncomfortable at first. Leads will be under-contacted, leaving hundreds of thousands of potential commission dollars on the table.

The mindset that you must adopt is much like that of a parent of small children. When these same agents were kids, chances are they were not fans of brushing their teeth every single morning and night. Still, someone forced them to practice the habit until it just became automatic. That's the same mindset you need to create in your buyer agents. Prospecting and lead follow-up is something that happens every day, just as surely as the sun comes up — and it's no big deal.

How to screw this up

Think of company-generated leads the same way you think of candy. In the right amounts, leads are fuel for hungry agents. Great leads can be used as rewards. But what happens when we eat too much candy? We become lazy and lethargic. The same is true when we get too many leads.

Agents can oversee about 150 leads at any given time and still meet the requirement to call them the 7+ times we know that it takes to convert the bulk of inbound leads that are actually closeable. On multiple occasions, I lost track of how many leads my agents were receiving, only to find out later that my agents were closing only the low-hanging fruit and letting the other leads wither on the vine. An excess of new business coming in each day makes lead follow-up unnecessary for those folks who just want to do a deal or two each month. The end result is a long list of leads that have been called only two or three times, despite being totally closeable. As a busy rainmaker, you'll be tempted to gauge the team's conversion success by the number of executed deals on the board. Look deeper in to the number of times each lead is called, and reward those folks who are doggedly pursuing their buyers.

I've Got Their Attention! Now What??

Establishing top-notch prospecting habits for your team is the basic challenge during Early Climb — but we've also got to make sure that we have powerful conversion methods to keep the prospect's attention once we've got it! Creating instant rapport and engagement with the prospect is both a science and an art, and mastering this skill is arguably the most important base to cover in the game of real estate sales.

There are some coaching programs out there with elaborate scripts for every possible objection, and prepacked responses for each flavor of response from the client. In my experience, that's an awful lot to remember on the fly, and the prospect generally knows when you're on a script versus when you're being authentic.

Build rapport by asking questions about the caller, occasionally pointing out a commonality that you share, and then bookend that with another question. Lo and behold, if you implement this simple approach with consistency you'll build authentic connections with the people on the other end of the line.

People will almost always choose to work with someone they like over someone who is obviously more competent but less likeable.

What you're up against is that sense of "stranger danger" that prospects have picked up from a lifetime of being oversold. Two to three minutes of laid-back conversation with a person who is generally interested in the answers will temper that physiological reaction that happens when we're contacted by someone we don't know. That initial jump in heart rate and blood pressure begins to subside. Now they can actually hear what you're saying. For a guide to basic scripting that actually works, go to bonus.wirbook.com.

Great phone conversations often result in excited clients booking appointments to either buy or sell a home. The general flow of a presentation, be it for a buyer or seller, is the same. You must first rebuild the rapport that you had on the phone (assuming you set the appointment for yourself). Nothing can proceed until and unless you ignite a personal connection with the prospect. Remember that people will almost always choose to work with someone they like over someone who is obviously more competent but less likeable.

Next you've got to qualify the client for their goals. Help them to articulate what they're really trying to achieve. What is going to make this effort a success?

Then you must establish yourself as the expert. Take them through national market trends, down to a regional level and then block by block in their neighborhood.

The next base to cover is differentiating yourself from the rest. Whether you are working with buyers or sellers, you can always find a way to address a pain point for the client in a way that no other agent has. For sellers you could use a "guaranteed sale" offer as a great way to demonstrate more value; for buyers you could promise that certain minor fees will be picked up by the seller or agree to cover them yourself.

Charge What You're Worth

If you choose to provide a premium service — an outstanding value that no competitor can touch — why wouldn't you price your product appropriately? If it costs you more to offer these added values, why wouldn't they affect your pricing?

Remember this: price is only a concern in the absence of value. If you've done a great job in presenting your value, the clients will be asking you, "How much is all of this going to cost me?"

For listings, create a commission menu with basic services and premium services that cost 1–2% more. Position the basic service, let's say a 6% gross commission, as the entry-level product. The best value option may be the 7% package, which includes many but not all of the benefits of the 8%, top-of-the-line service.

For buyer services, charge a transaction fee to cover the cost of delivering extra value to the consumer. You could even collect a check for the fee at the buyer consultation, as a way to help solidify the relationship between the client and the agent.

Net Promoter Score

In Early Climb, we are almost singularly focused on the prospecting actions (dials, contacts, appointments) that create revenue. But measuring the quantity of efforts up front without checking the quality of service on the back end is a mistake. Keep in mind that your online reviews are your report card for anyone who responds to one of your campaigns and decides to research your company before calling you. You can generate leads all you want, but if the service is poor, the reviews will be too. Count on an immediate dip in appointment conversions and a spike in cancellations if you receive a string of bad reviews.

To stay in front of this potentially lethal problem, implement a simple survey that asks clients to rate your team at closing. Send this to the settlement agent twice in the week prior to closing, and have all associates who attend closings keep copies in their cars as a backup. Your survey should ask your clients to rate their agent, and as your team grows, the transaction coordinator who helped with the file. It should also provide a generous space for feedback in paragraph form.

As the team owner, take advantage of the opportunity that the survey provides for you to create the final impression your company leaves on each client. If the feedback is glowing, capitalize on the opportunity to congratulate the client and thank them for the validation. Chances are that you're better at asking for referrals than your agents are, so use the opportunity to make that request of each client.

> *Customer service problems are like roaches... for every one you see, there are a dozen lurking in the walls.*

If feedback is negative, you should personally call the client to get more information on what your team could've done differently. Is the client justifiably frustrated with the way the transaction was handled? Did the agent drop the ball, and if so, how do you make it right? The broker who screws something up but owns up to a mistake is less likely to get a scathing online review.

Poor feedback on more than one transaction is a huge red flag that you should fire that team member. Remember that customer service problems are like roaches . . . for every one you see, there are a dozen lurking in the walls. Your marketing can be the best in town, but if you're not committed to delivering killer results every time, you might as well hang it up right now.

Emphasize Online Reviews

Hindsight is 20/20, and one of the habits I wished I'd developed earlier is the cultivation of a strong presence on the online review sites. There's a love/hate relationship with sites like Yelp that allow consumers to talk about their experiences with your company. On the one hand, reviews from the energetic raving fans of your service can provide enough firsthand credibility to motivate new prospects to contact your office. On the other, if someone has an axe to grind, you can be subjected to fake reviews from anyone.

More frustratingly, some review sites will ghost your positive reviews in favor of salacious reviews that get more clicks (presumably because drama delivers more engagement than ordinary thumbs-ups). There is rarely an appeals process for false reviews, and the courts seem to have determined that these sites have carte blanche to publish (or hide) any reviews that they choose.

Other sites are more even-keeled. Zillow will let you send your clients a link back to your profile so that they can easily review you, and Zillow will allow you to request that a moderator take a look at a questionable review that may violate the guidelines for submission.

It is worth noting that there are multiple services out there than can help you systematize the collection of online reviews. I can't recommend using them. Unfortunately, the review websites are generally opposed to these types of systems, and your account can be flagged and ghosted if they realize that you've employed one of these services. Instead, a very simple email script to your clients, sent out at regular intervals, can help to build a long list of reviews on any site you want. Check it out here: bonus.wirbook.com.

As the rainmaker, you should make a concerted effort to ensure that your past client testimonials are on every review site out there. You will also ask your new buyer agents (who have hopefully closed a few deals before) to have their clients review you on your company's profile. It's important that those reviews all go onto a shared team profile page. Five individual agent profiles with five reviews each don't make a big impression on a buyer who is clicking around on Zillow. But one profile with 25 positive reviews may be more likely to resonate.

Your new buyer agents won't have very many clients to contribute in the beginning, but over time their impact is phenomenal. New buyer agents tend to work with first-time homebuyers who are excited and appreciative of their agent's care and attentiveness, and they're uber-willing to write gushing testimonials to that point. Those are great reviews for your page!

The importance of these reviews cannot be overstated. It will do you no good to spend thousands of dollars on advertising if the first thing that comes up is a 1-star rating when someone searches for your company. The solution is to develop the right habits in Early Climb that will create a positive presence so that your marketing is even more effective when you transition into the more advanced stages of growth.

THE BACK OFFICE

We've established the importance of being laser-focused on recruiting talent and getting your first buyer and seller deals under contract. Revenue, after all, is king. To support all that new business, let's discuss some back office resources that you will want to set up in Early Climb to provide a foundation upon which your business can grow exponentially.

The Physical Office

If you are still practicing out of your home office when you start working on setting up your Early Climb pillars (tech, recruiting, etc.) so be it. But by the time you hold that first Buyer Agent Boot Camp, you need a professional space where your team can meet, train, and sit down with clients. The atmosphere needs to be comfortable but all about business. Even if you have a great house, your buyer agents are not going to be comfortable and productive in your personal space (and do you really want them there?).

Finishing out and furnishing a new office is not an option at this stage in the game. Sorry! So what's an Early Climber to do? You're going to get creative.

The solution you need at this time is probably not on Loopnet or listed with a commercial broker. Ideally, you need to rent space from another professional services operation. That space should come with access to printers, scanners, and at least one conference room (preferably more).

There are many more of these opportunities out there than you think. Consider the position of small business owners such as financial advisors or accountants. Their businesses' organic growth pushed them into renting and furnishing office space, but maybe with two offices in the back that are sitting vacant. At $20 per foot per year, that extra space isn't producing any income to offset its costs. You have an immediate solution to the problem. Pitch a month-to-month lease for $200–800/month (in an average small- to mid-size market). Offer to take possession immediately; the thought of receiving that additional revenue today is hard to pass up!

You can look into renting office space from a lender or title company, but the regulations around these arrangements can be prohibitive. It's up to you to figure out what will comply with any current rules, RESPA or otherwise.

Another viable but more expensive solution would be to rent an executive suite from an outfit like Regus or WeWork. Some of these companies have base packages that don't include an office with a door that shuts; I think these open space solutions are insufficient. You need a private space where you can keep client information confidential and phone calls discreet. Your buyer agents deserve a space where they can telephone prospect in a reasonably quiet environment. Again, the price tag on a setup like this is typically twice what you can negotiate with a small business owner who has extra vacant space, but it's a flexible option in case vacant space isn't around when you need it.

Legal

I recommend going to your local or state real estate commission and getting a list of attorneys who advise that body on things like contracts, litigation that affects agents, etc. (In Texas we have what's called the Broker-Lawyer Committee that advises our real estate commission. These attorneys are usually the most educated in the ins and outs of real estate litigation.) Contact the attorneys who sit on that board and find out who is taking new real estate brokerage clients.

You will want to have an attorney on retainer who can help you if you ever get into any kind of dispute between you and a consumer, or you and one of your agents, etc. You need someone who knows the real estate industry inside and out to advise you on anything compliance related when you run into one of these challenges.

Create a relationship with a second attorney who can help you with all things related to human resources. You will need a policies and procedures manual, which you can source from a cheap online template and then flesh out to fit your needs and situation. The attorney can review that for a relatively low fee. That attorney also needs to create or at least review your position agreements and addenda.

The third attorney you need will help you with the actual formation of your company. Whether you have just an LLC or an LLC with an S-Corp for tax purposes, you need an attorney who understands the pitfalls of setting these entities up incorrectly. The lawyer should specialize in this and do it all day, every work day. Or you could go the DIY route and use an online service to set up the LLC, but it's probably wise to have an attorney review what you've put together before it's actually filed.

If you were to open an office with partners (or add them at a later date), you will want the same attorney to break down for you all of the if/then scenarios involved in owning a team with someone else. If you're a single operator, things are less complicated.

Keeping Books

The next vendor you need to enlist is a bookkeeper. One of the biggest weaknesses that I see with small businesspeople in general (and real estate agents in particular) is that they don't know their numbers! This syndrome is especially bad in the real estate community among brokers trying to set up the team model. They're not tracking their expenses or using a standardized P&L and balance sheet to provide consistent financial statements. They fly by the seat of their pants; if there's money in the account, we must be good — right?

It's so critical to have a template you can use to identify all of your costs of goods sold and expenses. Categorize, for example, what the lead sources were for your particular transactions. You can track your turn-around investment and avoid spending money on lead-generation channels that don't produce.

A good bookkeeper can build that template for you and needs to be sending you P&L statements every week. Review them every Friday. You'll be surprised at how many costs you can cut to improve profitability! Ask for detailed expense and revenue sheets, which show you line-by-line where you spend your money and where your inbound closing revenue is coming from. You look to these reports to confirm the lead sources of where each actual closing comes from, so you can further validate the return on investment (ROI) for the particular lead source.

Expect to find a great bookkeeper for about $60-80 per hour, and initially you'll only need about two or three hours of bookkeeping per month. Keep this expense under $200 at this stage in your development. Expect that the bill will grow with your team's production, so you're probably looking more like $300–500 when your team swells to 20 people.

Next, you'll want to add a certified public accountant (CPA) to your back office team. Obviously this person helps you with preparing your taxes, but more importantly they can help you think strategically when it comes to business decisions that could affect your tax liability at the end of the year. Develop a mindset of always being on the lookout for potential cost savings, since those funds could be reappropriated to your lead-generation budget.

One thing that I'm sure you've noticed is that none of these players are being hired onto your team full-time. It's tempting to find a jack-of-all trades office manager to keep books and compliance in check. But that person will not be an expert in any of the bases you must cover with certainty. More importantly, you are in no position to take on the salary of an office manager in the Early Climb. Even if you could afford one, you won't have enough work to keep him or her busy full-time. Use contract labor and stay nimble!

Get Covered

As an owner of a real estate business, it's absolutely necessary to protect yourself in the event that you or one of your salespeople makes a mistake. **Errors and omissions (E&O) insurance is critical** to acquire in Early Climb. This might feel like a luxury item to worry about later, but trust me, it's not. If you or someone on your team makes a negligent mistake, you can file a claim against the insurance and be covered against the amount of the settlement and the attorney fees.

Operate without this insurance, and you run the risk of being sued and left to your own resources to defend yourself. Real estate litigation can leave you owing hundreds of thousands to the plaintiff and a similar fortune to your attorneys (and possibly the plaintiff's legal team as well). You could end up owing enough to wipe out your net worth in one fell swoop.

It's not a matter of IF litigation will happen to you; it's a matter of WHEN. At the level that you're going to be producing, **it's a statistical certainty that at some point you will be sued.** Go ahead and make peace with that fact now. You'll have some transaction where, whether your agent was at fault or not, you and the agent will be named in a lawsuit.

I've surveyed dozens of attorneys who represent people in the professional services space, and they all say the same thing: if you're running a really good business, you're holding people accountable and hiring the right people, you're still going to average about 1 out of 1000 transactions that involve an E&O insurance claim. It's possible to obtain a $2 million policy very affordably by accepting a $5000+ deductible. You can usually score E&O insurance for $50–100 per transaction closed; a small price to pay to have peace of mind that you won't have to shut your doors because of litigation.

The Virtual Assistant

Simply put, a Virtual Assistant (VA) is an assistant who can work from anywhere and never actually shows up to your office. (I've been working with my first VA for five years and have never met him in the flesh.) The benefits of going virtual are mostly about cost-savings.

Virtual assistants work from places like the Philippines, Panama, and other countries. You could opt to work with someone who is stateside and works from home; however, I recommend you explore the overseas option at this stage in your development. Currently, you can get a great virtual assistant for about $8/hour from vendors like MyOutDesk. The vendors contract with the VAs and act as middlemen, providing candidate options for you and training for the VA, as well as coaching, management, and terminations should the person not work out.

So what all can a VA do? Here are just a few ideas that a VA could handle for you while you're prospecting or out in the field making money:

VIRTUAL ASSISTANT TASKS

- Manage your email inbox
- Create property flyers
- Create activity and website reports for sellers
- Create activity and website reports for vendors
- MLS entry (if allowable in your area)

- Third-party site management (Zillow, Trulia, etc.)
- Listen to and grade buyer agent performance on lead calls
- Direct lead traffic between buyer agents
- Call on your behalf to set up or cancel appointments
- Call for customer feedback
- Send out requests for website reviews
- Manage social media profiles

The virtual nature of this work (and the fact that offshore VAs won't understand local stateside real estate markets) limit them from serving as a fully functioning executive assistant (EA). Rather, the VA will come to serve at the direction of the EA.

Because of the strength of the U.S. dollar, $6–8/hour goes a lot further in developing nations than it does here, and it provides a great life for our VAs. Before you object to sending an American job to a foreign country, I want you to think of it this way. If you don't hire a VA, you should keep doing these things yourself. In a few paragraphs, we'll talk about beginning the hunt for the right executive assistant (EA). You need help right now on the reactive stuff that eats up a lot of your time; you can't wait for the EA hire. (And when you make that hire, the EA will have more important work to do than creating property flyers.) The virtual route is the only way to make the numbers work at this stage and still get some help RIGHT NOW.

To find the right VA, reach out to companies like MyOutDesk and ask them to introduce you to VA candidates who have worked in the U.S. real estate industry in the past. Great VAs should have no problem referring you to the brokers they worked for, and you'll call and verify with those brokers that any candidate you're looking at did a good job and caught onto tasks quickly.

Interview at least 10 people. Factoring in VAs' personality and core values is much less important than with other hires, as they almost never interact directly with clients. Ideally, your VA has a history of working for one company for an extended period of time. A VA who jumps around every three months can create a future problem for you.

TIPS FOR SUCCESS WITH A VA

- **Check the internet connection.** In the U.S. we take for granted the access to reliable, affordable broadband internet. In other countries, the service is less consistent and may be subject to caps on the volume of data that can be transferred. Ask your VA candidates about any limitations on their data plans, and have them send you screenshots of their results from SpeedTest.Net.

- **Be incredibly clear about your expectations.** Most VA's I have worked with are trained to execute orders exactly as given; no more, no less. Create a document that details the base-level procedures and instructions for subsequent if-then scenarios.

- **Rigorous training up front will save you loads of time down the line.** Your VA is working at a disadvantage when compared to in-house employees, who have the benefit of observing you operate and hearing you solve problems yourself. Make sure that you block off enough time to teach the VA the skills necessary to perform well, and give feedback freely to help your VA get it right.

- **Require your VA to keep a record of his or her daily activities** and report them to you at the end of each day. Adjust the workload accordingly. One of the challenges of having an assistant who works remotely is that you aren't able to easily observe whether the VA is actually working. This makes it hard to gauge available VA bandwidth.

- **Leverage video and internet voice service** to create more of an in-office presence for your VA. If you have an extra PC or tablet lying around, you could use it to keep an open video connection via Google Hangouts (assuming the VA's internet service supports this). That virtual presence can help to integrate your VA as a true part of your team.

Courier, Photography, and Staging Services

Even in Early Climb, you're going to need to contract with a courier to deliver signs, lockboxes, and flyers. If you are working a very tight geographical area that has virtually no traffic congestion, you might be able to delay this expense. You may be forced into using professional courier services at this stage, but ideally you would find a dependable high school kid with a pickup truck who is over-the-moon excited to earn $25 for putting a sign in the yard and flyers in a box.

Professional photography services are a must, even if you were a great photographer in college. You need someone who has wide-angle capabilities, who understands architectural photography, and who is adept in Adobe Photoshop as well, as almost every photo will need to be enhanced in some way.

You should be able to find someone to provide these services for $100 per listing. If you develop a relationship with the right photographer, you may be able to negotiate that they also deliver your sign and temporary flyers at the time of the initial shoot, which will cut down on your courier costs. You may want to choose a photographer who can do aerial photography as well, if you work in mostly higher-end areas. If not, make sure you have a backup photographer who can do the aerial and/or 3-D tour photography in case you do obtain a luxury listing.

The last vendor to create a relationship with is the **home stager.** A few years back, home staging courses were all the rage, and tons of people flooded into these certificate programs only to find that the market for home staging was quite limited. The result is that home stagers, even the good ones, work very affordably. You should be able to hire a stager to perform local consultations for $75, including providing the homeowners a list of suggested changes before photos are taken. Home stagers may also offer full staging services (with furniture they either own or rent) and can upsell your client on those services if the client desires.

The Executive Assistant

As we've established, erecting the Seven Pillars is impossible to do all by your lonesome. You need a right hand to help your left execute on the big promises that you're about to make to your agents and clients alike.

All hell is about to break loose and you will drown in a fiery lake of missed calls, half-finished projects, and pissed-off people if you don't get some help.

Now is the perfect time to run ads and hold interviews for your first salaried position, the **executive assistant** (EA) role.

Hiring your EA is last thing you'll do in the Early Climb. In the interests of keeping your costs down in this bootstrapped phase, you're going to want to hold off for as long as you can before making this hire.

This person will be key in setting up your back office systems and helping you with time management. I remember the anxiety of hiring my first W-2 employee. *What if I hire the wrong person and burn a mountain of cash in the process? What if my listings don't sell and I can't pay salary?* I get it, but here's the deal. You will stay stuck at this production level if you do not make this key hire, and do it now. Spoiler alert: All hell is about to break loose and you will drown in a fiery lake of missed calls, half-finished projects, and pissed-off people if you don't get some help.

In our model, your first EA is a jack of all trades. When I think about a Fortune 500 company, at the top they all have a Chief Financial Officer, Chief Operations Officer, and Chief Technology Officer. Your EA has to wear all of those or manage outside contractors who cover those bases for your team. (In the Teenage Years, it's essential that your EA is an energetic problem-solver with mad Google skills, as the goal is to minimize the amount of external help required.) Your EA will be working with a bookkeeper and an accountant, managing your transactions, and serving as the first line of defense for contract and compliance questions from your soon-to-be buyer agent team.

When you move to recruit an executive assistant, I suggest that you target a specific market first: paralegals! These folks are typically very structured, detailed, and organized. Most importantly, they know how to take massive action. They can produce a significant amount of work in an eight-hour period. I've found tremendous success in sourcing people from the paralegal world, and their salary expectations are generally in line with what an EA should earn.

As the transaction coordinator, your EA will need to be a licensed real estate agent and comfortable not just with numbers, but also a natural at dealing with clients. There will be times when the EA will cover your closings, write listing agreements, and negotiate repair amendments. Your EA should excel in areas where you are weak. He or she needs to anticipate your needs, remember what you're likely to forget, and fill in the gaps.

Your position as rainmaker has you holding one listing presentation after another, while managing marketing campaigns and training buyer agents. Calendar appointments and seller callbacks fall through the cracks. A good EA helps you keep your focus — and your promises.

Exhale. Doesn't it feel good to have a plan?

What Lies Ahead

Remember that in the Leadership & Scaling section I told you to hang onto that SWOT analysis? Go ahead and pull it out now. Review the seven pillars of your business and use this chapter to create a strategy for establishing a foothold in each one of those areas of success. Break each strategy down into actionable goals and realistic but aggressive timelines for each key thrust. These are called your **tactical operating priorities** (TOPs).

Transfer these commitments to a calendar, tape them to your bathroom mirror — whatever you need to do to keep them front and center. Exhale. Doesn't it feel good to have a plan?

Congratulations! You've just set up your real estate team, Version 1.0. Hold onto your hat, because Early Climb is an exhilarating time that can also be turbulent and painful. The struggle of setting up systems and making your first hires is soon followed by a period that can be incredibly fun. You will help people succeed, even some who have struggled before in real estate, and you will compete with the establishment brokers and WIN! Deals go under contract, your buyer agents become largely self-sufficient, and your virtual assistant remembers your spouse's birthday and orders flowers based on a calendar reminder. This is the part of Early Climb that I call the Ignition.

But . . . (there's always a but).

You can't just stay in the fun and excitement of the Early Climb. If you've built your seven pillars as I've prescribed, then you've already created the momentum that will push you out of Early Climb, whether you're ready or not.

You're about to enter the next phase in your development, and there will be bumps along the way. But on the other side of this is a well-oiled, incredibly profitable real estate business that can grow as quickly as you can keep up.

CHAPTER 3
The Awkward Teenager

I want you to think back to when you were 13 years old.

If your adolescence was anything like mine, you experienced an awkward phase that made it seem like everything about you was in some state of transition. Uncoordinated, gangly limbs cause you to trip and fall and, for us guys, our voices croak like frogs. Your nose grows before the rest of your face can catch up; you're covered in acne . . . but luckily everyone is too distracted by your headgear to notice.

Close your eyes and really remember what it felt like to not yet be an adult but know that you aren't a child anymore. Feel that angst and frustration. The freedom of adulthood is on the horizon but still decidedly out of reach. You are impatient and irritated that you can't just shortcut to living like a grownup.

The next stage in your business's growth is a lot like being an awkward teenager. Your team feels like it's getting stuck in the mud; problems emerge that you don't have the time or capital to address. You're outgrowing your systems, and last week you got your first negative online review. The cracks begin to show. You have too many listing appointments and you're dropping the ball on key service delivery items. The buyer agents start to feel ignored and adrift since you've gotten so busy. And your personal life isn't great either, since you've been neglecting the home team to keep this circus going.

LEADERSHIP AND SCALING

Moving into the Awkward Teenager phase isn't so much a decision; it sort of just happens to you as you become a victim of your own success. Now you're tasked with pushing through this, which is painful, or staying stuck at this size, which involves just adopting chaos as a way of life. There is clear path of escape, but you can't begin your march until you're totally prepared.

So what's the plan for moving your business into the next stage of growth? Why do we have to be so deliberate here? Because to build enough velocity to escape the crushing gravity of these problem-riddled, challenging months (or even years), you'll need to grow your team in all directions.

You'll be growing your staff to handle back-office operations, as well as developing your leadership for the sales teams. You'll pump up your marketing with mass-media options and the addition of an inside sales agent.

You're probably adding up the costs as you read along. The Awkward Teenager phase is all about laying the foundation for Explosive Growth, and that means onboarding the players and systems that make it possible for you to double and triple your business over the following one to two years. But identifying and training all of the new talent required to support that growth, as well as writing massive checks for advertising that will inevitably take months to deliver break-even returns . . . well, it can feel like rolling a boulder up a steep hill. Hands down, this is the least rewarding stage and easily the most anxiety-producing.

Throughout this process, you'll notice that you're repeatedly firing yourself — over and over, you'll seek out someone who is better than you are at conversion, coaching, or detail work, and you'll delegate those tasks to an expert. This can cause a bit of a head trip as you learn to relinquish control, allow these folks make their first mistakes (sometimes rather big ones), and celebrate when they produce results that are superior to what you could've accomplished in your days of managing those same tasks.

How do you know when you're ready?

The first step is to read this whole chapter. Create a spreadsheet of all of the key thrusts that you're going to implement while in the Awkward Teenager phase. Do your research and come up with safe annual cost estimates for each of those items. Take the total, divide by 12 and then multiply by three. That's three months of your new, heavier operating expenses that MUST be in the bank, unless you're doing mass-media advertising and sending a listing partner out on the appointments.[4] (We'll get to all that in a second.) As long as you're the one still going on listing appointments while you're running mass-media ads, you need only three months since you're operating at a higher profit margin. I recommend the rainmaker (that's you!) go on mass-media-type appointments — those expensive ones you got from radio and TV spots — for six months to a year to keep profit high and give you the cash to reinvest into the business to grow faster by adding better lead generation and key operational staffers.

The second item you need to satisfy before moving forward relates to your listing inventory. You should be booking enough appointments that you are listing no fewer than six new properties each month. On your FSBO/expired/withdrawn appointments, you should produce a 30% conversion rate MINIMUM — otherwise, you need to further sharpen your saw when it comes to your presentation, as well as your follow-up on those appointments that don't sign a listing agreement on the spot. If your conversions aren't above 30%, you're not ready to push forward with more expensive seller lead sources.

The third requirement involves your buyer team's phone conversion skills. Are the buyer agents following your script training and objection handling?

---

[4]This estimate pertains to your operating income, which is separate from your living expenses. You should have six months of living expenses in the bank at all times.

Are they conducting themselves in such a way that you can relax, knowing that your company is being well represented on the phone?

If you've checked the boxes by all of those items, then it's time to move forward with the solutions that will propel you closer to your Great Escape!

THE SALES TEAM

In this stage, your sales team will undergo a radical transformation. The fledgling team of agents that you built in the Early Climb has matured into a group of confident, competent salespeople who represent your company well. As the associates improve their conversion skills and transactional knowledge, natural leaders will emerge. These are the folks who will one day help you lay the foundation of a sales machine that produces profits whether or not you're physically in the office.

Yes, you're embarking on a challenging period of changes and growing pains, but this is a profoundly exciting time in your development. You'll work your ass off, get kicked in the teeth a few times, and build strong bonds with your team members in the process. The uphill climb of the Awkward Teenager phase is where you find your tribe — the loyal true believers who have truly bought into your vision.

WANTED: Kirk Seeks Spock

Are you a fan of the Star Trek movies?

Even if you're not, surely you're familiar with the relationship between Captain Kirk and his right-hand man, Commander Spock. Kirk's modus operandi was all about big risk, big reward; he was perpetually thinking outside the box to beat the bad guys and save the day. Mr. Spock, on the other hand, was the logical, steady first officer who made sure

DESPERATELY SEEKING
SPOCK

Me: A visionary leader, a man with a mission—and the will to make it happen
You: The one who has the smarts and steadiness to keep the mission on track and moving forward

Together, our enterprise can live long and prosper.

that Kirk's wild ideas didn't get everyone killed. Mr. Spock knew everything about how the ship worked (maybe more so than Kirk) and captained the ship while Kirk was on his wacky away missions.

Come back to this century for a moment. Chances are that, if you're reading this, your personality type trends toward the D (dominant) on the DISC assessment. It's not universal, but D's tend to make up a majority of the hard-charging, risk-taking visionaries that are motivated by the kind of growth potential that we're discussing in this book. (I think it's safe to assume that Captain Kirk was an off-the-charts D himself.)

I've heard the real estate business described as a "cult of the D," meaning our industry worships this personality indicator and values it above all others. There's a lot of logic behind that assessment, as results-oriented D's will push a business forward in ways that other personality types probably won't.

But what the collective industry mindset ignores are the many and varied shortcomings of the driver personality. D's are often impulsive and impatient, not to mention resistant to compliance and detail. To a classic high-D leader, the thought of managing and teaching a revolving door of agents on the same, repetitive challenges probably sounds like a *Groundhog Day* nightmare. They are perpetually distracted by shiny objects and are keen to start projects that never get finished.

High-D personalities like yourself are typically excellent "empire builders." The missing piece is an "empire protector." You need someone who can grow with you and bring a steady, stable layer of leadership to your bucking bronco of an organization.

What you need next is a good **buyer agent team leader** (BATL).

By this point you will have trained several classes of buyer agents. Some worked out; others didn't. If you've remained disciplined about your prospecting for sellers, then you've created a ton of appointments and are spread too thin to properly oversee your buyer team. One thing is certain; you are not as available and effective at supporting the team as you were a few months ago.

Step back and take a look at the team you've built. When you're not around, who do the other agents ask for help? Which agent seems to have invested in working for you long-term rather than treating your company like another stop along the way? Who knows the most about how your systems actually operate on the back end, or who would be the easiest to get up to speed on those items?

What I'm asking is, who's your Spock?

In the Awkward Teenager phase, your right-hand operative will take the form of a great BATL.

BUYER AGENT TEAM LEAD TASKS

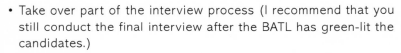

- Train buyer agents on prospecting, lead role plays, and review call recordings
- Review offers and coach agents through transaction process, amendments, etc.
- Take over part of the interview process (I recommend that you still conduct the final interview after the BATL has green-lit the candidates.)
- Handle corrective action plans for buyer agents, firing underperformers as needed
- Serve as your surrogate in the office while you're in meetings, working with vendors, etc.
- Handle client complaints and service escalations for buyer team, as well as the listing team when you're not around

If you really pushed yourself when recruiting buyer agents in Early Climb, you should have no problem identifying the person who wants to be with your organization for the long haul and in whose hands you would feel totally comfortable leaving control of the ship. If you made a mess of hiring buyer agents early on, then you may not have anyone on your team that fits the bill. Junk in, junk out.

Here are some other characteristics to look for:

BUYER AGENT TEAM LEAD CHARACTERISTICS

- Technologically proficient; can learn basic functions of any software system easily
- Patient, since they'll be taking over the buyer agent training and coaching
- Able to lead and motivate agents and to hold them accountable
- Respectful of compliance with systems and contracts alike
- Experienced, with at least 25+ transaction sides
- Natural problem-solving skills, with a calming, reassuring effect on clients

Hiring the right person for the job is crucial; you can't fully devote yourself completely to building a killer marketing machine and a massive listing inventory until you know that your buyers (and agents) are in good hands. Support your BATL when needed, but allow autonomy on most decisions. Be clear with your expectations, the realistic goals you've set, and the key performance indicators the BATL needs to report to you each week. Expect that there will be a learning curve and mistakes in the beginning. Give general guidelines on how you want things done, and then **get out of the way**. Let your BATL run with it. It's his or her job now; you're fired.

One effective way to compensate this person is by offering an override of 5% on the buyer agent team commissions. You could also structure things so there's a modest salary and a reduced override percentage, or salary with an override that excludes the first five or ten buyer agent closings.

Just as you hire your buyer agents with their future growth in mind, so will you promote this person with the idea that BATL is the first upward step of many. Hopefully you've identified a person who can grow into an executive role from the BATL position.

Find Your Phone Ninja

While we're on the subject of firing yourself from some key parts of your business, let's talk about another major pain point that you've experienced in your role as Captain Everything during your Early Climb days.

Would it be fair to say that, on occasion, you let your other commitments encroach on your seller prospecting time block? The brand ambassador candidate who can only meet at 9 a.m. or the seller who won't stop texting during your dial session — it's like they're all conspiring to derail you from your mission to build a rockstar listing inventory. Heck, sometimes you're a victim of your own success and don't have time to prospect because of all the appointments you've booked!

Would it be fair to say that, on occasion, you let your other commitments encroach on your seller prospecting time block?

Would it also be fair to say that after months and months of hammering the phone for expireds, withdrawns and circle prospecting leads, you're kind of sick of the phone? Maybe some of those intruders could've gone without an immediate callback, and subconsciously you let them get in the way because the distraction provides a welcome sense of relief. In fact, you've noticed that you have to psych yourself up more and more each time you sit down for a dial session. You can do it, but sometimes you wonder for how much longer?

Phone prospecting can be more draining than any other activity in your day.

Phone prospecting can be more draining than any other activity in your day. There's something about the adrenaline of the chase that can leave you with a bit of a hangover from all of those fight-or-flight chemicals bouncing around in your system after hours of power-dialing. Things would be different if you could put your feet up after a hard morning on the phones, but you have too many demands on your time between clients, vendors, and a new BATL who's just now getting up to speed.

So fire yourself.

I'm next to certain that there is someone out there in your city who is a better phone prospector than you are. There are plenty of folks who make their livings working a dialer for all kinds of industries, so the well of talent to draw from is quite deep. We call these folks inside sales agents, or ISAs. (Check with your jurisdiction to see if they also are required to hold a real estate salesperson license in order to call and book appointments for you.)

This role is a dream come true for talented salespeople who find our industry exciting but want their evenings and weekends to themselves. An experienced phone salesperson is used to spending long hours on the phone. Then they get to leave work at a predictable hour or after reaching their goals for calls or appointments set.

A few characteristics that make a stand-out ISA include:

INSIDE SALES AGENT CHARACTERISTICS

- A patient, curious mindset with the capacity to remain genuinely interested in the prospect's story, even if it's on the last call of the day

- A secure self-image and a high threshold for rejection

- Artful management of time on the phone and the ability to maintain control of the conversation's direction; graceful exits when the lead is not qualified

- An ability to shake off a bad call and quickly get in the right mindset to dial again

- The certainty that the work is helping prospects move forward with something that they want to do anyway and that is in their best interest. This helps when overcoming reflexive objections from apprehensive prospects.

- Humility—the willingness to not play the role of the expert but, rather, defer to you and your team as the authorities on real estate questions

The compensation for this role can vary widely, so check out the other inside sales opportunities on Indeed.com and Craigslist.org to glean what a going wage is for an experienced ISA in your area. The most confident and motivated ISAs will be fired up by the idea of going straight-commission and earning a lucrative override on each deal closed as a result of their efforts. However, the reality is that even rock stars have obligations and need a certain degree of predictability. Be open to offering a modest salary or, as a third option, a contractor arrangement combined with an initial draw to help the ISA through the early months of pipeline-building.

Optimize Your Sales Bench

Look around your office and take stock of your human capital. Who are the future leaders? Who are the long-term utility players? Which struggling but dedicated agents may work better in a support role, when the opportunity presents itself?

Take an objectively critical look at the buyer agents who are underperforming. Be rigorously honest with yourself about which agents are striving to improve, and which are settling into a comfortable mediocrity. You will probably find that some of the least productive agents demand the most of your time and resources. Which agents tend to disappear for days at a time, always with an excuse for bailing on their prospecting? Which agents show up every day but will do anything to creatively avoid making phone calls?

Be rigorously honest with yourself about which agents are striving to improve, and which are settling into a comfortable mediocrity.

Think about the new buyer agent team lead you're hiring; do you want that person to spend time on the agents who don't really want help, or would you rather the BATL focus on moving obstacles out of the way for your real go-getters?

This assessment is more difficult than it sounds. You've worked in close quarters with these folks and care deeply about their successes (and egos).

You may feel a special affection for them since they took a chance on you in your Early Climb, and I definitely understand the loyalty. But remember this: this relationship you have with your agent must be mutually beneficial or it needs to be dissolved. An agent who is ignoring leads is not contributing to the team's success and is actually hindering it by allowing those marketing dollars to fly out the window and underserving potential clients.

Cross-Train Your Agents

You will probably choose to remain the listing agent-in-chief through the Awkward Teenager phase, and that can be a smart move. Toward the end of this stage, however, you should create some redundancy by encouraging your more experienced buyer agents to develop their listing chops.

I'd predict that there's an 80+% chance that your first full-time listing agent (coming soon to an Explosive Growth team near you) will be a trusted and talented person whom you originally recruited to your buyer specialist team. I would encourage you to let any agent practice for a full year as a buyer agent before trying out the listing side. Let's consider Agent Tom. Tom has been a great buyer agent, but you need to really see that he shares your zeal for serving the client and that he has experienced the most common transactional challenges so he will be prepared for sellers' rapid-fire, left-field questions.

Role play the scripts and objection handlers with Tom and then drag him along with you to see a few listing presentations. Then, it's time to see him in action. This time, you'll be shadowing him while *he* presents to sellers and handles their comebacks.

A good application of his new skills would be to handle a few appointments each month, mostly the overflow of what you can't (or don't want to) handle. This arrangement also gives you cover should you need to pop out of town for a few days.

Agents appreciate being trained for listings, and more importantly, the opportunity to advance their careers. One thing I've learned is that to create a happy staff and team of agents you must provide them something to work toward. With few exceptions, almost everyone wants to feel like they're moving forward in life.

How to screw this up

Failing to provide feedback when a star performer stumbles is another pitfall. I hired a buyer agent once who was a real go-getter in his first year with our team. We talked about future team leadership opportunities. He would've been a natural at the elements that make for a killer BATL. Then he had some shifts in his personal life. He stopped showing up regularly and his client service slipped. When a team leadership opportunity opened up, I promoted someone else. The agent came into my office, angry that I hadn't asked him to interview for the position. Everyone, including the agent, knew that he wasn't a viable candidate given his unstable performance. Still, the last expectation that I set was that he was on a path for a leadership role. I messed up when I didn't communicate to him directly that his trajectory had changed.

TECHNOLOGY

The great thing about all of that hard work that you put in when setting up your website and other tech tools way back in the Early Climb is that all the heavy lifting is already done. The middle stage of your development just involves some technology tweaks. If you're itching to take on massive tech challenges, don't despair, as you'll undertake a total technology revamp as you enter the Explosive Growth phase. But let's not borrow tomorrow's trouble today. Let's go over a few simple upgrades you can make during the Awkward Teenager phase to improve your technological prowess.

Nerds Make the World Go Round

In the Awkward Teenager phase, your business is simply not profitable enough to hire someone to administer your technology full time. Your buyer agent team lead may or may not be able to fill in the gaps when it comes to troubleshooting hardware and software issues. A great solution for the Awkward Teenager phase is an IT services contractor.

The scope of work that this contractor needs to be capable of depends on a couple of things. If you are still in a co-working environment or leasing space from a group that provides the networking for printers and internet, then you can probably get away with an informal contract with a smart student from the local college's computer sciences program. This person should be capable of helping to push your agents and staff past low-level software challenges (like "my computer has a virus," or "I can't connect to the internet") and light maintenance and upgrading of hardware.

If, on the other hand, you alone are responsible for delivering printing and internet services, you're going to need more specialized help. You need an on-demand network administrator. The standard fee in the Austin, Texas, market is roughly $120/hour. That hourly rate feels like a punch to the gut, I know. But think about the cost of your downtime, which only grows as your operation expands. Four hours of no internet can kill the productivity of your paid W-2 staff, combined with untold costs of missing leads and dropping the ball on service delivery.

I recommend aligning with an established outfit for this gig. You should interview several to make sure that it's a long-term fit. This contractor might charge a little more, but if you switch providers you will be utterly at a loss when the new administrator asks you a thousand unanswerable questions about how your ports are configured (unless you are also, by chance, a tech genius yourself).

Upgrade Your Google Game

At some point, your business will outgrow the individually owned (and free) Google accounts. The primary pain point here is a lack of control when it comes to storage of files and emails by your employees and agents.

Consider the eventuality that an agent quits unexpectedly and two months later there's a question about whether he or she actually sent an important disclosure to a client. You don't own that free Gmail account, so how would you access the emails if the agent won't cooperate? Heaven forbid that something happens to one of your agents and you have to pick up a transaction right in the middle of escrow. How would you know what's been taken care of and what's outstanding?

Right now you're using the free Google Apps suite to run most of your email, calendar, and file-storage functions. But for roughly $10/month per user, you can gain control of inbox archives, file storage rights, and contact lists, as well as have Google host your email server (so you can use a professional email address as your actual login instead of an @gmail.com account). At the time of this publication, there is a cheaper option available, but we prefer the $10/month upgrade plan that includes the email vault and unlimited storage, which eliminates the need for third-party solutions like Dropbox. The pro version also comes with actual human support, versus the largely self-service support of a free Google account.

The Landing Page

For our purposes, let's define a landing page as a very simple website that tries to get you to provide your email address and other information in exchange for downloading a free ebook or special report, etc. (The technical definition is broader, but 99% of the landing pages you visit follow the simple recipe I've just described.)

Landing pages are often built upon a single call to action. There is usually little else to click on; the goal is to get the prospect to provide the one thing you want — contact information. When that happens, the landing page displays a thank-you page, which tells the prospect how to collect the free item. The item could be delivered via a hyperlink, a direct download, or an email.

Prospects are then added to your database and can be put on an email campaign that automatically touches them with prepacked content relevant to the same subject matter as the original item of value. You can test two offers side-by-side (called A/B testing) to see which offer produces more results.

You could code all of this by hand, but I don't recommend it. There are several different solutions that use templates to create very slick pages that convert at a high rate. LeadPages (lp.wirbook.com) is a great value and probably the easiest option to master. You can connect it to just about any email marketing or content management platform in a few minutes and you're done.

Raise your hand if you somehow used brute force efforts to produce 30 deals a year at a big-box broker, made it all the way through the Early Climb, and still can't say with a straight face that you have your database organized?

Deploy a Stock CRM

In Early Climb you cut your teeth on low-cost marketing for both buyers and sellers, and succeeded well enough to create the champagne problem of having too many leads to manage. But in a few short paragraphs we're going to talk about scaling up your marketing to a level you probably never even considered possible. You're going to have a well-oiled buyer agent team and a shiny new inside sales agent (ISA) to handle the wave of inbound inquiries generated by all of your advertising avenues.

The lead-management system that comes with your property search site will handle the leads well enough for the time being. But what happens once you've earned their business? How do you collaboratively manage the transactions, and how do you keep up with your clients after the sale?

Raise your hand if you somehow used brute force efforts to produce 30 deals a year at a big-box broker, made it all the way through the Early Climb and still can't say with a straight face that you have your database organized?

You're not alone. Maintaining a spotless and well categorized database of contacts is the central core of basic agent training wherever you go. But the natural tendency for a lot of you high-producing sole operators is to keep it all in your head. But consider this an intervention — a natural point to pause and take remedial action to get your database in order.

Straightening out your database doesn't have to be painful. You can enlist the help of your VA to go back through your emails and start creating contact record entries in your Google Contacts, and using the context of the emails to classify each as a client, a lead, a vendor, or a personal sphere contact. It's easy to tag each contact on one or more lists. Those contact lists can then be exported to a CRM (Customer Relationship Management) tool. For new contacts, develop a habit of recording home purchase anniversaries, birthdays, and notes about anything potentially relevant later, such as their favorite sports teams and restaurants. The best CRMs will allow you to create custom fields to import whatever information you want.

Once those lists are complete, it's time to export them to .CSV files and get them into the new CRM. When it comes to the choice of CRM system, I want you to give up on the dream of a perfect CRM system right now. This is not your long-term solution. You need, over time, a solution that will grow with you, and none of the off-the-shelf platforms will, I'm sorry to say. For now, you need a temporary solution that will maximize the referral juice in your database, as well as allow your team to collaborate on your transactions.

It does not need to be perfect. You can use something as simple as Insightly, TopProducer, or the like. I like Brivity for its robust, real estate-specific features, and frequent updates. When it's all said and done, you're going to have to migrate to an enterprise-level system when you move into Explosive Growth; you're going to outgrow the capabilities of any of these real estate–specific solutions and need something that helps you run all areas of your business, not just your client database.

MARKETING & LEAD GENERATION

In the Early Climb marketing section, I emphasized the necessity of keeping the lead-acquisition costs as low as possible. In the Awkward Teenager phase, we're going to flip that on its head. Full disclosure here — I'm going to present the roadmap that created massive success for my team in Austin. You need to assess the market where you practice to see if some of these marketing channels are already saturated or, for some other reason, not viable.

Remember that in the introduction, we went over the fact that you're going to have to reinvest a significant amount of your revenue back into the business? Well, we're at the point where the costs of progress go way up, and some of the checks that you'll be cutting are not for the faint-hearted. Keep in mind, though, that there is a significant time savings when we talk about these types of advertising outlets. After a little upfront work of writing the ads and getting voiceovers just right, these campaigns run themselves with very little of your attention required. Contrast that with calling FSBOs, door knocking, and the time-intensive marketing tricks of the Early Climb, and it's clear that you're recapturing a significant number of hours every single week.

Inbound leads aren't cheap, so I have to reiterate here that before you roll out these campaigns, your ISA and Buyer Specialist Team must be ready. They need to be ninjas at scripting and handling objections before you open the floodgates of expensive media leads.

Before we dive in, an important note: advanced marketing is a risky proposition. You MUST study your market to ascertain whether any of the marketing channels that I'm recommending here would have legs in your market. One or more of these tactics may be completely saturated in your marketplace; an entrenched competitor may suck up all the oxygen in a certain space, so it's about finding a pond that hasn't been overfished. Considering getting a pair of experienced, fresh eyes to review your strategy (and one that doesn't have a marketing product to sell you).

What's Your Hook?

The broad exposure that mass-media radio provides will accomplish the simple goal of getting you in front of thousands of potential new customers. Leveraging the listener's relationship with the longtime hosts will lend a credibility to your claims that you wouldn't otherwise have. But that's only half the battle. What messages can you deliver that will motivate those prospects to pick up their phones and call you?

You need to identify and cultivate a hook, an offer that is so interesting that the listener can't help but want to know more.

You need to identify and cultivate a hook, an offer that is so interesting that the listener can't help but want to know more. The hook needs to instantly communicate massive value to potential sellers.

One unique selling proposition (USP) that we've used with loads of success is the Guaranteed Sale Program. Simply put, the program provides a backup solution for those sellers who are concerned that their property will not sell within a specific period (or not at all). As part of signing a listing agreement, we work with the seller to pre-negotiate the price, terms, and timeline in which a partner entity can purchase the home if it fails to sell on the open market.

It's important to note that the success of such a proposition depends upon having an experienced, high-skilled salesperson handle the appointment. These are often very experienced sellers who are calling, and they're walking into this appointment with a certain degree of skepticism about your USP. In the example of the Guaranteed Sale Program, you've got to be able to articulate very clearly to the seller that this is a break-in-case-of-emergency solution, and that you're working in their best interest to sell their home conventionally and for top dollar. You are NOT there with the intention of buying their home at a discount. Share your exhaustive marketing plan to further demonstrate that you're pulling out all the stops to get them an offer on the open market.

This program is not a wholly new idea, as brokerages across the country have implemented the same call to action. There tends to be a lot of skepticism about this type of offer, so it was really important for us to make sure that we implemented the program with transparency and that all of our listing agents are able to communicate the terms clearly and effectively.

The promise of a guaranteed offer may not be the right unique selling proposition for your market. The timing may not be right for this kind of advertising hook either, since in a sustained seller's market, people are much less concerned about not receiving offers on their listings.

Other impactful propositions could include "easy-exit" listings that have simple cancellation policies if the client is unsatisfied with your service. Showing the clients a lengthy and incredibly thorough marketing checklist at the appointment can make a big impression as well.

I recommend you get some help with your strategy from someone who can help you determine which USP will return the best results in your marketplace.

Hire a Media Strategist

This stage in your marketing development is all about going big. In my opinion, the costs involved with this expansion are too heavy to use a DIY approach to strategy and implementation. I can't recommend going it alone.

A good media strategist will assess the efficacy, pricing, and saturation of your advertising options, as well as your operation's readiness to handle the influx of business. Media strategists help you negotiate the best spots and endorsements, and the fees they collect are pennies compared to the money you can easily waste without a solid strategy in place. Good media strategists want to produce excellent results (so you'll keep paying them!).

The best media consultants won't take your money if the time and opportunities aren't right. In 2010, I called the number-one media consultant in the real estate industry. I called to solicit his services in handling a media campaign for my then-fledgling brokerage. He stopped me mid-sentence, asked a few key questions, and flat-out told me that I wasn't ready.

I'm pretty sure that if I would've gone directly to the media outlets, they would've been more than eager to take my business, create some mediocre spots with no real direction, and cash the checks while I struggled with little or nothing in the way of results. I always feel like I dodged a bullet when the consultant turned me down, and so I used the bootstrap marketing of the Early Climb to build a team ready for the spotlight. We circled back in early 2012, when the team reassessed our business and decided that we were prepared to handle the increased volume. They created a kick-ass strategy that allowed us to dominate radio in the 11th largest (and fastest-growing city) in the country.

Hit the Airwaves

Radio is brilliant for lots of different reasons, but I think my favorite is how much control it gives you in targeting a certain demographic. The age range where we find the most homeowners looking to sell happens to be 45 to 65 years of age. These folks are not using digital music delivery as much as millennials are (who turn on Pandora and Spotify to hear whatever they want to hear); instead, your targets are listening to FM radio — and probably to the same morning show that they've been listening to for the last 10 to 20 years.

There are statistics that your media strategist can use in choosing the stations and shows that will deliver the highest return. Cumulative weekly

> *Your targets are listening to FM radio — and probably to the same morning show that they've been listening to for the last 10 to 20 years.*

reach is a leading indicator; timeslots with higher reach will cost more. The size of your market can drastically change your costs as well. In a metro area like Austin, Texas, you've got a population of just under two million people. Your typical spot on a prominent station is going to run anywhere between $175 to $350 per 60-second spot. In smaller markets of 250,000 people, those costs could drop to $50 to $75 for the same 60 seconds, while mega-markets like Los Angeles can charge anywhere from $500 to $1200. Your consultant can help you figure out whether the number of leads created is worth the acquisition cost.

The listeners who are dyed-in-the-wool fans of the morning shows hold those hosts in high esteem. They've heard these hosts every day in their cars for possibly decades, and have established loads of credibility during that time. Booking endorsements with these hosts can be the key differentiator for your radio campaigns. Leveraging that respect can have a huge impact on how likely the listeners are to pick up the phone and give you a call.

There are often multiple hosts on these shows. You need the person with the biggest personality and that people find the most entertaining. Choose the host who isn't the energetic and influential character, and your campaign will fail.

How to screw this up

In Austin we had a very popular radio personality who left his loyal audience on the pop station to move to the country station. We advertised with him right after the switch and ended up wasting tens of thousands of dollars. Two years later we came back and tried it again, and this time around the campaigns actually produced leads.

Trust is built over time with an audience, and it's trust that gives prospects that extra push to actually pick up the phone and call you. Stick with radio hosts who have been on the airwaves the longest on your market, preferably on the same station for 10 or more years.

You want this person to personally endorse you and talk about the clients you've served who were directly referred to you by that specific personality, and who also heard about you on the radio. The juice is in reading the testimonials, your unique value propositions as a team, and getting the personality to energetically read the endorsements live during peak drive times, whether it's the morning drive or the long commute home. (Radio tends to deliver the greatest impact in the suburbs, since advertisers have the opportunity to get a message to commuting listeners over and over again.)

Here's an example of a great live-read endorsement we use here in Austin:

This is Brad Booker with Mix 94.7. I just got an email from another listener who recently worked with Chris Watters of Watters International Realty. This lady just told me that she had her home previously on the market with another agent. For over SIX MONTHS, the house failed to sell. She was super-frustrated. She was under contract to buy another home and lost her earnest money on that deal, costing her thousands of dollars. She missed out her dream home because her old house failed to sell. She heard about Chris here on Mix 94.7 and she heard me talking about him. She called Chris. Chris put his marketing machine to work in advertising her property for sale. Within three days, Chris got this lady an offer above asking price! Can you believe that, three days and he listed it for the same price as the previous agent who tried to sell it. If you're thinking about selling your home, hire the only agent I would use. Chris Watters guarantees to sell your home. You don't have to be worried about being held to a long-term listing agreement. If you're unhappy at any time, you can fire him. Don't forget that he has his Guaranteed Sale Program, where he guarantees to sell your home at a price and a deadline you've both agreed to — or he will buy your home for cash. If you're interested in selling your home, call the only agent I trust. His name is Chris Watters and you can call him at 512-212-1221 or visit www. guaranteedsaleaustin.com).

Most agents who try radio advertising want to voice the commercials themselves (for either ego or cost-saving reasons). This approach seems to fail more often than not.

The other mistake that agents make most often is not hanging in there long enough for the campaign to work. Your cash-conversion cycle on radio is going to be a minimum of six months to break even. Let's say that your six-month campaign costs are estimated at $50,000. Be prepared to kiss that money goodbye and not look back. You're in the campaign for the long haul, or you shouldn't be in it at all.

Why does media advertising take so long to deliver results? You're programming thousands of listeners with top-of-mind awareness that triggers them to think about your company when they think real estate, but this process requires a ton of repetition. Plus, the needs of the average seller are rather immediate, but you have to wait for those opportunities to pop on their own timelines — the advertising just increases the chances that they'll call you when the need arises organically.

If the six-month cash-conversion cycle makes you nervous, here's some perspective. Direct mail, a longtime staple of real estate marketing, takes 12 months minimum to break even, on average. (One of the best direct mail marketers I know said it took him 18 months to get out of the red ink on direct mail in his suburban submarket.) Not to mention, there's always a chance that you've missed the mark when it comes to what areas to seed with direct mail. You may choose an area with more competition than you estimated. Remember that volume ebbs and flows in each area, so a neighborhood that experienced a wave of turnover this year may see almost no movement next year.

Radio is a totally different beast in terms of quality of leads and the ease of conversion. For example, you could spend $3000/month and generate a total of 15 leads. That leaves your lead cost at $200. The difference is in the conversion, as those 15 leads can yield you between five and seven listing appointments. We're talking about a 30% to 40% conversion rate from inbound calls received to actual listing appointments set. Fast-forward to the actual listing appointment and you'll find that the conversion from appointment to signed listing agreement is much higher as well. In my experience, two out of every three radio listing appointments you go on will convert into a signed agreement.

In the end, radio will have between a 6:1 and 7:1 ROI. That doesn't even include any buyer-side deals generated from sellers who are selling to buy another property. One important caveat: if your team isn't already doing $30M+ in gross sales, you will likely not see this kind of ROI. It will be significantly lower, maybe just a break-even proposition. Once you're at about $30M+ in annual sales, you'll have enough transactions going on in the marketplace and signs in the ground (key!), which will help you increase overall top-of-mind awareness. If I haven't scared you away from doing radio after reading this and you decide to test it with a skinny listing inventory, or without a media consultant, just write a check for $50,000 and send it to your favorite charity because that money is about to burn up in flames.

This same brand awareness helps with conversions on your outbound prospecting. Prior to mass-media exposure, nobody knows who you are. You're calling expireds with a variation of the same script that every big-box agent is spewing. It's really hard to differentiate yourself when your scripting is the same as the competition's. But with your new radio exposure, now you can say:

Hi, my name is Chris Watters and I own Watters International Realty. I'm calling because we're looking for our next testimonial to share on the morning talk show on KLBJ-AM. We'd love for you guys to be our next success story. When would be a good time for me to sit down and share with you all how we've helped countless people just like you? In the past we've featured homes like yours on the morning talk show for more exposure. Those homes had previously failed to sell and we got them sold quickly. What times work best, mornings or afternoons?

Media and Recruiting

Obviously, mass-media outlets are going to introduce your company to thousands of folks who wouldn't have otherwise heard of you. But there are benefits beyond the leads and opportunities created by some of these sophisticated marketing campaigns. The mass-media advertising creates an unbelievable amount of brand equity in the real estate community. Most agents who've tried radio ads, for example, don't employ the right strategies or they don't hang in there long enough for the ads to work. If you're the broker who finally cracks the nut of making this kind of advertising work, you will earn a lot of respect in the real estate community. Think of how much easier this would make your recruiting? The immense credibility created will multiply your efforts when prospecting on agents to join your team.

Some of my very best hires were agents from outside our area who heard about us on radio. These folks have experienced success as lone-wolf agents in another market. They have a heightened appreciation for all of the leads that our advertising provides because their top concern is that they've walked away from their personal sphere and are starting from scratch in our market.

These agents are savvy enough to want to instantly align themselves with the brokerage that delivers the most leads. If they're from out of state, they're also concerned about compliance since each state varies so much when it comes to transactional process, contracts, and special concerns. They don't want to go into a big-box brokerage model where the agents are unsupervised (until something goes terribly wrong). It just makes sense all around for them to join a team that has the opportunities, brand recognition, and credibility that they can utilize on day one. This was a great and unexpected benefit that I observed after starting our media advertising assault.

Advertorial Content

Have you ever seen, in a magazine or newspaper, those columns that look like the rest of the magazine's content except for a small note at the top that says "promotional" or "advertising"? Occasionally, I'll read those sections (mostly when I'm stuck on a plane and have forgotten to bring a book). But mostly I dismissed those opportunities as "people never read that stuff...." Shockingly, I found an application of this

> Be careful spending money on print advertising; but apparently it is not as dead as we've been led to believe.

technique that was one of the most effective and affordable media marketing tools and one that I wish I had discovered much earlier.

Our local newspaper has a beautiful real estate–centric insert in its Saturday editions. I was approached by the newspaper to create some of this content (called "advertorial," as it straddles the line between advertising and editorial content). I worked with a writer to create a few pieces that focused on our listings, market conditions, and other real estate trends. I was surprised, but it did make the phones ring the following Monday.

Be careful spending money on print advertising; but apparently it is not as dead as we've been led to believe.

USE MEDIA ADVERTISING FOR SELLERS ONLY

One of the hard-learned lessons in real estate radio advertising is that, in general, marketing to buyers just doesn't work. As we discussed earlier, the needs of a seller are more immediate, and that urgency creates the extra oomph needed to convince the prospect to call your office. Sellers always have one or more pressing problems to solve, like a career move, divorce, or outgrowing their existing home.

On the other hand, the conversion cycle of a buyer is usually very casual; coming around to the idea of buying a home (or moving-up) typically falls much close to the "want" category of purchases vs. an actual "need." The leisurely, fun process of home shopping makes it very difficult to capture the attention of these laidback prospects with even the best buyer-centric USP.

Become Unavoidable with Retargeting Ads

Tell me if you've ever had this experience. You're shopping online, maybe checking out some T-shirts on Amazon or the like, and you decide not to purchase. Instead you bounce to your local TV station's site to read the news, and then maybe catch up on a favorite real estate blog. Strangely, the TV station's website and the blog both display ads that show the T-shirt you were just checking out! How did that happen?

I'll spare you the convoluted and very technical explanation of how those ads are delivered back to your browser even though now you're on a totally different website. These are called retargeting ads and they allow you to take advantage of recorded web history to make your ad pop up again and again to those folks who have already demonstrated at least a mild amount of interest in your content.

We have two retargeting ads, one for buyers and one for sellers, and we display them depending on what type of site the prospect came in on. You can use one of your USPs as the headline or maybe a link to a white paper on something like "Seven Costly Mistakes That Home Buyers Make in Austin" or "Questions to Ask When Interviewing Real Estate Agents." You could have these ads link back to landing pages where the prospect can download the white papers and also search for homes, or submit their information for a free home valuation.

The setup for retargeting ads is probably better left to the professionals who know how to make sure that they appear in the correct context. Check out Redline Digital Marketing, which handles our campaigns. You can learn more about them at rdm.wirbook.com.

Spiff Up Your Collateral

For in-person appointments with prospects, it's important to have some basic branding items on hand that echo the credibility and professionalism that you're communicating with your advertising and online presence. Don't go overboard; a few essentials will suffice.

> Koozies, pens, and T-shirts are fun, but they offer almost zero return. Save those items for when you have money to burn!

I think that folders are essential. You can get some great, durable plastic ones with your company logo very affordably through online providers. These become very practical for listing appointments and buyer presentations. You can standardize your agents' listing presentation packages, for instance, by having an assistant fill the folders with the relevant documents. Prepacking buyer presentation folders can help to ensure that your important disclosures make it to the meeting table, and it gives a nice takeaway item that can sit on the prospect's desk (and remind them to call you back!).

We tortured ourselves for months, trying to find an affordable solution for printing professional-looking buyer guides and other marketing pieces. Eventually, we found that the best solution was a cheap and cheerful coil-binding machine that we found on Amazon.com for about $125.00. You can build slick reports with clear plastic covers and black plastic backing for about 45 cents each, and any buyer agent is capable of using the super-simple binding machine.

I am not a believer in frivolous spending on branded giveaways. Koozies, pens, and T-shirts are fun, but they offer almost zero return. Save those items for when you have money to burn!

COACHING & TRAINING

At this stage in your team's development, the pace at which you're launching new initiatives can be dizzying. Every week finds you stretching your time management to its limits. But this stage also marks an important shift in your mindset. You're taking the first major step toward business ownership and away from the Captain Everything mentality. By delegating the bulk of your coaching and training duties to your new lieutenant, you free up the space to focus on building a killer listing inventory and creating the revenue that allows you to build out the team required to succeed at a high level. Your Buyer Agent Team Lead (BATL) can provide the reinforcements that you need to keep your business marching forward on its way to Explosive Growth.

Set Higher Standards

In addition to assuming the responsibilities of trainer-in-chief, your BATL must become your accountability officer. The BATL's first task may be a bit of damage control in this department, as the competing demands on your time in the Early Climb don't usually leave enough time for you to implement consistent and thorough monitoring of the agents' key performance indicators (KPIs).

Speaking of those KPIs — what does accountability look like in a world of 1099 contractor agents? Start with your initial covenant. Build into the independent contractor agreement a minimum number of transactions per month required to stay on your team (after a reasonable grace period for ramping up), and spell out what happens when an agent falls below that production level.

Set very clear expectations for the additional KPIs that you expect the agents to meet on an ongoing basis, such as minimum standards for the number of dials and live contacts made, as well as appointments set. The BATL should be reporting to you weekly on his or her KPIs. The BATL can provide these stats on a paper tracker or use Google Forms to input KPI data every morning (for the previous day). For demonstration purposes, I've created a very simple starter form for your agents to use in reporting their call activities. You can download it with the other freebies at bonus.wirbook. com.

The parallels between parenting and managing agents are many.

Your exposure to the buyer agents should be limited in general — they need to graft onto the BATL as their leader; if you don't make this separation, you'll still be answering contract questions at 9 p.m. on Saturday nights. Discuss the importance of enforcing boundaries and responsibilities with your BATL, as you both need to be committed to upholding the same standards or it won't work. (Does this sound familiar to those of you with kids? The parallels between parenting and managing agents are many.)

The BATL should not only record and report these stats but also audit each agent's self-reporting for accuracy and, occasionally, play the role of investigator if it looks as if an agent is fudging numbers.

If you receive pushback from an agent regarding the accountability standards you've set for the team, consider this a pulsating, red-alert warning that you've almost certainly made a poor hiring decision. Agents who resist transparency and oversight entered the real estate business for reasons that are incompatible with your organization over the long term, probably for the flexibility and personal autonomy. Such agents are highly individualistic, with a self-congratulatory internal narrative, but their actual results, invariably, are lazy and inconsistent.

Improving Call Quality

One of the most challenging aspects of running a buyer agent team is providing a consistent, professional response to inbound calls. Internet leads and sign calls should be going directly to the sales agents. Those agents will inevitably have different levels of experience and lead-handling skills, which means that training them to handle inbound lead calls is crucial before you turn them loose to represent your company on the phone.

A schedule of clearly defined phone shifts gives ownership to one or two agents. In Austin, we carve up the day into three shifts per day between the hours of 8 a.m. and 9 p.m. and have two people on each shift (since multiple calls tend to come in at the same time). Set the expectation that during phone shifts, agents should be in front of a computer and in an environment that is quiet.

By the way, the requirement that agents be stationary for phone shifts becomes feasible when your buyer agent team hits about seven or eight agents total. When you started the Early Climb, your team consisted of just two or three buyer agents, making it nearly impossible for an agent to be at a desk for every shift (since that equates to 30 to 45 hours of desk time!).

Part of your BATL's weekly reporting should include reviewing inbound call recordings for compliance with the training you've provided in the areas of scripting and objection-handling. Using a system like CallRail (callrail. wirbook.com) will allow you to receive instant emails with links to the recordings, so your BATL is able to forward examples of calls that were handled ideally (or give feedback on those that don't go so well). The recordings relieve you of the responsibility of "secret shopping" your agents on the phone, since you get to hear how they actually talk to real clients.

Don't let this fundamental quality control measure fall to the bottom of the priority list. Your new BATL may initially be overwhelmed by the long list of new responsibilities, but this is one basic check that must happen continuously. The agents need to expect that every call is being listened to and graded; skip this step and I guarantee your call quality will go from mediocre to cringe-worthy in no time.

Don't send your radio or other seller-gen campaigns to the buyer agents; your ISA is a much better choice for qualifying those leads. In the absence of an ISA, book them yourself.

Systematize Your Training

As the rainmaker of a team in the Awkward Teenager phase, one of your responsibilities is to equip your BATL to efficiently train class after class of agents who know how to sell and will represent your company well. But once the team exceeds a handful of agents, your BATL's list of responsibilities can swell so large that time available for training new recruits is reduced. Training buyer agents properly is a time-intensive and repetitive endeavor. How can you improve the efficiency of the training process and redirect your BATL's time toward more dollar-productive tasks?

Training buyer agentsproperly is time-intensive.

Since the nature of basic agent training is so repetitive, consider a solution that allows your BATL to teach each class once — instead of once a month. By creating quality recordings of both core classes and special training topics, you and your BATL can build a library of raw video tutorials on basic items like "How to Fill out an Offer" and "Role Play of a Buyer's Presentation." These files can live on your shared Google Drive, in a folder dedicated to training videos. Name each lesson clearly so that the trainees will be able to locate the file they need quickly.

In the Explosive Growth phase, we'll use a special tool to organize your lessons and track agents' progress through the courses. It's an investment that I think can wait until then, because right now the most important thing is recording the content and having an easy way to disseminate it, which your unlimited storage on Google Drive provides.

Your BATL also needs to compile a training checklist that addresses all facets of a new agent's education. The training sessions should be very focused on intense sales training early on, with ongoing trainings moving forward. New agents typically want to immediately explore the transactional process, technology toys, etc., but the thing that is going to make them (and you) money quickly is learning how to convert leads to appointments over the phone. Plus, you don't accomplish anything by teaching contracts to a new agent who has no clients to speak of. Instead, adopt a just-in-time training approach that teaches each area of the business on a schedule that follows the typical agent's progression. Here's a simplified outline of a sample introductory training program:

TRAINING PROGRAM: A SKETCH

- Week 1: Tech tools, basic scripting, and objection handling. Heavy role play and prospecting.

- Week 2: More prospecting and role play. Introduction to buyer's presentation and transaction process.

- Week 3: Outbound prospecting, introductory training for handling inbound calls. Buyer presentation role plays.

- Week 4: Booking appointments from inbound calls. Overcoming appointment objections. Purchase offer basics.

If your training is recorded to video, your BATL can leverage those lessons to create a self-directed curriculum with very specific objectives for your buyer agents to check off the list and report back. Here's a snippet:

SAMPLE BUYER AGENT TRAINING CHECKLIST

☑ Listen to successful, recorded in-bound calls. Role play similar calls with Team Lead. If Team Lead gives a passing score, then Virtual Assistant will add you to inbound lead rotation. _____ (BATL initials here)

☑ Scan MLS and identify one bank repo open house opportunity. Schedule bank repo open house, or traditional open house if no foreclosure opportunity is available.

☑ 30-dial call session

☑ WATCH: Preparing for Appointments: Buyers' Financial Motivations

☑ WATCH: Preparing for Appointments: Pre-qualification vs. Pre-approval

☑ WATCH: Preparing for Appointments: Property Showings — Best Practices

---

You could also consider investing in a coaching company to coach your BATL through implementing accountability strategies and training plans. The BATL won't need it forever, but there are some great programs that help leaders get their feet under them and build confidence in their mentorship abilities.

BRAND AMBASSADOR PROGRAM

We might be in the Awkward Teenage phase of your team's development, but this is the time when your Brand Ambassador Program (BAP) really starts to hit its stride. In Early Climb, building the BAP can be a bit stressful since you, as the rainmaker, feel pressure to deliver results for your partners immediately. In the middle stage of your development, your partners have already benefited from your Early Climb marketing and are now reaping the benefits of your new initiatives.

Don't be discouraged if you had a false start or two with vendor partners.

Don't be discouraged if you had a false start or two with vendor partners who weren't ready to commit, or whose situations changed and are no longer able to contribute to the co-marketing budget. Relationships with your existing partners are going well and about to get even better as you get ready to deliver additional value to their businesses.

Start Your Vendor Roundtable

The attention that you're able to help direct to your vendor partners is the first level of value that you can provide — and essential to cementing the relationship early on. But over time, the focus shifts. The real juice in the BAP is in the mastermind group of business owners that you've assembled.

Put together a monthly meeting of your vendor partners. It might be hard to get buy-in at first, but trust me, once you've held a few of these meetings your BAP members will be bugging you about scheduling the next one! For the first meeting, it's really about having each partner go around the room and give their elevator pitches (you only have to do this once unless you're onboarding a new partner that month). You want to help hard-wire connections between the vendors so they are encouraged to trade referrals peer-to-peer, in addition to any business they might receive from your clients. As the glue that holds this new group together, you'll play the role of moderator during these sessions (which is a lot more fun than it sounds!).

Each meeting, every vendor will answer couple of key questions:

- What are you doing right now that's working really well?
- What are your greatest challenges?

The partners are learning from each other; they share some of the same pain points and are all at different stages of development. One partner will share that he is excited about trying newspaper advertising, causing another to share her experience in finding out which types of ads work and which don't. As business owners, we've all tried things that didn't work. Sharing that knowledge says "I've been through this lesson already. I've paid the tuition. Here are the results, free of charge."

When you started your BAP, you had to convince vendors to join. If you provide this level of value, word will get out and you'll have a waiting list of business owners who want to join.

Be the Hero

One of the biggest surprises for me as the moderator of the vendor group was how many of these successful vendors were working at a deficit when it comes to marketing, recruitment, and processes. These business blind spots have left these business owners effectively fighting with one hand tied behind their backs. It is a testament to the quality of the services they provide that, despite these challenges, they've created as much success as they have.

This is an area where you can have massive impact for your BAP members. Marketing and technology tools that you take for granted are revolutionary in the eyes of the owners of service businesses who have built their businesses almost entirely on past client referrals.

For example, one of my vendor partners, Tyler, wanted to grow his business. He had experimented with advertising before and had a vague sense that it might have worked, but he had no idea how to track the results (he didn't even think to ask the leads "How did you hear about us?"). I showed Tyler how he could nab a cheap tracking number that would ring through to multiple salespeople, provide recording

It just never ceases to amaze me how many successful business owners are missing out by not leveraging smart, affordable tools to push through their challenges.

functionality, and even show up on caller ID as the tracking number (so his sales team would know that it's a very expensive warm lead calling). He was astonished; you could see his wheels turning, connecting the dots on the new possibilities.

To be clear, in no way am I picking on Tyler. This guy busted his ass for fifteen-plus years to get where he is now, and he's earned every client the hard way. It just never ceases to amaze me how many successful business owners are missing out by not leveraging smart, affordable tools to push through their challenges.

Let's stay with Tyler's situation for a second. Where else could you add big value to his business in a way that is also easily automated and low-cost for you? You're already paying for a call-capture system; I can think of a long list of service providers who could benefit from having a "recorded line info" option to help hook callers who aren't ready to talk to a live operator. Use your account to set up an extension, and point the notifications for that line to the owner's sales team.

Here's a way to go really big with your value proposition. This would work best as a benefit for partners at a higher contribution level, since it's more of a time commitment. If you've subscribed to a landing page service like Leadpages (and plan to remain a subscriber over the long haul), you could host a conversion page that offers a white paper specific to the vendor's business, like "Seven Things You Should NEVER Do to Your Lawn," or "How NOT to Get Ripped off When You Buy Insurance." Then you could help the vendor get a Google AdWords account to help advertise the fancy new page.

If you really LOVE helping people, this work can offer a huge emotional payoff as well.

OK — one more! (I get very excited about this topic — can you tell?) These business owners are, at least from a marketing and back office standpoint, stuck at the level of sophistication that your operation was at the beginning of the Early Climb. They are bogged down every day by repetitive, reactive tasks that aren't where business owners should be focusing their time. The same Virtual Assistant (VA) solution that took the pressure off the valve for you will help these owners keep it all together as well. Labor cost is always the barrier that keeps these folks from hiring the help they need; you are able to help them find a killer solution.

Yes, by going the extra mile for your BAP members, you're creating stickiness within the group and reinforcing your bottom line with their marketing contributions. But if you really LOVE helping people, this work can offer a huge emotional payoff as well. I can't tell you how energizing it was to see the instant relief on Tyler's face when he realized that, in a few minutes, I'd just helped him solve a problem that he had no idea how to tackle. It is totally expected that your vendor partners will end up implementing your suggestions and seeing an ROI of 100X what they're contributing each month.

Ninja Tactics Vendor Results

Like I said, it's really fun to help these BAP members get creative about their businesses. Let's discuss some advanced techniques for helping your vendor partners boost their sales.

Many of your partners offer services that are linked to the real estate business in one way or another. Plumbers, electricians, and other home service contractors are accustomed to receiving direct referrals from agents. But there's a second tier of opportunity up for grabs as well.

Think about the expired, withdrawn and FSBO listings that have failed to sell this year or the long-term actives that are currently languishing on the market. If a home doesn't sell, it's likely that there's a problem with condition, either cosmetic or fundamental in nature, that is to blame. This could create a big opportunity for your partners, if they want to take the initiative and drum up some business. You can distribute a list of these failed listings and their addresses (assuming it's OK with your local MLS).

Let's say that we're dealing with a flooring contractor. A vendor could divide the failed-listing list among her salespeople and then door-knock the homeowners of an expired listing. She can contact the homeowners and create an estimate for new flooring if it seems like old carpeting is turning off buyers.

What's going to happen is that the property will eventually come back on the market with a new agent. Ideally, the seller would utilize our vendor partner to complete the upgrade. But even a seller who can't afford to make the repair could laminate the estimate and post it on the dining room table, along with sample color choices.

What does this accomplish? Buyers would be able to see that the repair is affordable and is no reason not to buy the home. Having a competitive quote on the dining table advertises the vendor to every new buyer and buyer agent who tours the home. The new buyer may negotiate for the seller to repair the flooring using our partner or may employ those services after closing. The worst case is that your vendor's marketing gets in front of a few dozen sets of eyeballs they wouldn't have encountered before.

There's another idea that we've used with much fanfare from our agents. There are home service vendors who can save the day at the end of a complicated transaction. Tell me if this has ever happened to you: a seller has no money to repair a home. There are defects that are intolerable to the buyer or, more often, the lender. If the appraiser notes a significant issue with anything from flooring to foundation, the lender's underwriting department will treat these notes as gospel. If the appraiser's suspicion that there's a defect is correct, the loan is dead until you satisfy the lender that the repairs have been completed.

But again, the seller has no money, and let's assume that the lender will not allow an escrow holdback because of the nature of the defect. The only way you can get the transaction across the finish line is if a vendor does the work without being paid up front. Instead, the vendor secures the work with a lien against the house. (Check your jurisdiction for any relevant rules, and the vendor should be directed to consult with an attorney who can explain the process and risks.)

The solution offers a huge win/win for the vendor, the clients, and you as the agent. Your home service vendors can develop this line of business. They can market to agents, lenders, and title companies so that when this kind of issue pops up organically, your vendor is the go-to person with the solution.

BACK OFFICE

Your executive assistant (EA) is likely to be feeling the burn from the bump in business you've created through your marketing efforts and relentless prospecting. Besides keeping your sellers happy and informed, your EA is tasked with wrangling a random array of admin tasks like running payroll, paying contractors, and feeding financial information to the bookkeeper. The back office pillar in the Awkward Teenager phase is mostly about providing assistance to you and your EA in the form of listing service delivery, and also in providing predictability on your team's financial health.

The Listing Manager

Between taking care of keeping your head on straight and keeping listing clients informed and satisfied, your EA can't do it all. Executing expert service delivery on the listing side involves tons of detail and repetition. The next full-time hire that you need to make is the Listing Manager (LM).

Your LM should be an experienced taskmaster, ready to implement the same checklists over and over on new listings that come in — and with a high tolerance for executing repetitive tasks that would become too tedious for most people. (On the DISC profile, a natural style of SC—steady and conscientious — is strongly preferred.)

Your LM will also work closely with your Virtual Assistant (VA) to execute the exhaustive checklist of marketing items that you've promised to the seller. This hire helps establish the architecture for the listing team moving forward. Your EA interfaces with the client and negotiates with buyer agents, while your LM delivers on marketing logistics and the VA handles things like designing flyers and creating a strong internet presence for each property.

 If we drew this process on paper, what we're describing would look similar to an assembly line. This is an important point, and I want to share a hard-won lesson from our experience in the Awkward Teenager phase.

In our group's development, we launched major media marketing initiatives and doubled the volume our group produced in the span of one year. Our service delivery process organically developed into an assembly line model, which would have been fine — except we made a near-fatal mistake. We had every person along that assembly line interacting with the clients, because more is more when it comes to communicating updates — right? We were so focused on keeping the clients informed every step of the way that we created a wholly separate problem. The clients found the communication from different sources dizzying; even though we outlined in the listing appointment who the players were, sellers were confused and told us that they preferred hearing from only the listing agent with whom they originally met, and a max of one assistant.

After taking our licks from a few frustrated sellers, we changed our process so that all communication funneled through the listing agent or the EA. One small change that we implemented with success was using the EA's email account to send out updates that were actually being produced by the VA or LM. This works well as long as all of those parties are in sync about what messaging is going out to the clients. (If the EA sends sellers an email saying that their home is live in MLS but seems surprised by that fact when the seller mentions it on the phone a little later, you're in trouble.)

During Explosive Growth, the EA will no longer facilitate transactions; a new player will take over the role of coordinating each file and communicating with the clients directly.

See Around Financial Corners

The Awkward Teenager phase starts after a certain degree of hard-won success in the Early Climb. The new revenue obviously helps with the large sums that you're investing back into the business via marketing and new hires. But playing with greater stakes requires that you pay even more attention to your cash flow than before. Your financial picture is now too complex to leave totally in the hands of a CPA and a bookkeeper.

> I'll tell you who you need: a part-time CFO on a contract basis.

I'll tell you who you need — a part-time CFO on a contract basis. I would be willing to bet that if I took a group of successful small business owners and asked them what a CFO does, 80% wouldn't be able to say. If you google the job description, most CFO tasks may seem unimportant for a small company. However, at this stage in the climb, a CFO's job is basically to help you understand what's going to happen in the future and forecast future profit and loss statements. Effectively, the CFO helps you see around corners by projecting the financial outcomes of the future as determined by the decisions that you're making in your business right now. As a business owner, it's really important that you understand how that proposed advertising campaign will affect your profitability over the next three months. That's a critical edge that you need when deciding whether to pull the trigger on that new spend.

Besides marketing, the other impact zone where your part-time CFO can help you make decisions is in hiring. Your new labor costs are second only to advertising in terms of sheer dollar amounts. Those costs can have a huge negative impact on core capital. The ability to predict the coming months' finances can help you decide with confidence whether you're able to make new hires or keep your existing staff if the market softens.

The typical cost of a contract CFO is around $180/hour. A cool thing is that a CFO can log in to your QuickBooks account, review your numbers in real time, and then build cash-flow models to help you make important decisions quickly. You might pay the CFO for 10 to 15 hours up front, but after that, you're looking at an ongoing expense of four to five hours per month, max.

Whew—are you looking forward to moving out of the Awkward Teenager phase yet? If you're feeling a little dazed after going through all those nuts and bolts, I totally understand. But it's going to be worth getting through all this, because if get the Awkward Teenager phase right, you're primed and ready to embark on Explosive Growth. The next chapter will show you how to navigate the challenges — and enjoy the rewards — that are coming.

CHAPTER 4
Explosive Growth

I can remember a period in junior high when our class received monthly visits from a Texas state trooper. The officer was intimidating, despite wearing a wide-brimmed hat that seemed comically big for his head. He visited our classroom and spoke to us first about self-esteem, then quickly segued into educating us on the dangers of drugs and gangs.

What stands out in my memory of everything he taught us was that to join a gang, you had to be "jumped in," which means the rest of the gang beats you up pretty good and that's your initiation into the family. Then, if you ever wanted out of the gang, you had to be "jumped out," which involves the same beating, but this time it buys your ticket out of the group.

In hindsight, this very linear process sounds a bit too clean and organized to be the standard operating procedure for every band of juvenile delinquents across the nation. The imagery here is so reminiscent of what it's like to work your way through the Awkward Teenager phase. It's hell going in and it's hell coming out. But then you're free.

Surfacing from the depths of the Awkward Teenager stage and into Explosive Growth is a near-magical time. If you're approaching this process in a way that's mindful and aware, you may even see the shift happening around you, as opposed to being able to only identify it in hindsight. What I mean is . . . enjoy it if you can, instead of thinking later, "Oh yeah, THAT'S when everything got better!"

> The Awkward Teenager phase: It's hell going in and it's hell coming out. But then you're free.

LEADERSHIP AND SCALING

How did I know when my team had hit the Explosive Growth stage?

The answer is complicated only because so many elements of my business showed drastic improvements all at once. Because we tweaked our listing processes, our sellers felt more secure, which lifted our net promoter scores drastically. Our buyer agent team benefitted immensely from its new team leader getting his feet under him, which also allowed me to be out of the office working on high-level marketing projects and converting listings. The new media campaigns took a few months to produce results, but when they did, they hit big and at a time when I had the bandwidth to close them. Our executive assistant and listing manager both saw gains in efficiency, cranking out more files than I thought possible.

If you follow through on the heavy lifting and smart investing of the early and middle stages, it's going to pay off. For us, it ignited, and we went from producing about 150 transaction sides to 325 in about 12 months.

So, it's working — you're firing on all cylinders. Now what?

Surprise! It's time to grow again. This time will be less painful. You're out of the weeds and into the gravy; the new hires you'll make and systems you'll deploy are the next dominoes we need to knock down to get you closer to your Great Escape.

First, you're going to begin your graceful exit from your role as listing agent superstar. You're also going to recruit for new talent to carry some of the burden. Then it's time to flesh out your support team and take a big leap toward creating a technology platform that helps to run your entire business. You'll take better control of your buyer leads and leverage a few smart resources to cut your training costs and retain talent.

THE SALES TEAM

Topping the list of sweeping changes in the Explosive Growth phase is the growth of the sales team. You may personally find this change to be quite difficult if you've always identified as a salesperson first and a businessperson second. You've already chipped away at the unmanageable list of responsibilities you owned when you were Captain Everything — but the biggest shift is yet to come.

Fire Yourself from Listings

The most basic core competency of any real estate team that's built to last is its ability to secure a reasonably steady stream of new listings. The listing agent is the lynchpin of the operation. That's a hat which, heretofore, has rested squarely on your head and your head alone. For you to ever make a Great Escape, we have to change that.

Chances are that you are great at getting listing agreements signed. You may even find meeting with sellers energizing and somewhat addictive. If you absolutely love listing appointments, I'm not going to tell you that you absolutely must give them up forever, but you will need to let someone else take the reins for a period of a year or so while you build out the rest of your operation.

There are a few characteristics to look for in a rockstar listing agent (LA). At the end of the day, it's the LA's knack for walking away from most listing appointments with a signed agreement that makes him or her indispensable. But what good is conversion if there's no follow-through?

A candidate for the LA position must have done at least twenty transactions before being considered for the role. Do not, under any circumstances, send a brand-new agent out in the field to represent your company on company-generated listing appointments. Without the procedural chops acquired when handling buyer-side transactions, you can count on that agent to make

> *Show me an agent who delivers great service to the customer, whose past clients are died-in-the-wool Raving Fans, and I'll show you a highly empathetic person who cares deeply about creating killer results for clients.*

unfulfillable promises and muff the answers to the sellers' questions.

Sellers, as we've discussed, are more intense than buyers because of the pressing and sometimes problematic nature of their needs. They're much more likely to interview more than one agent for the job, and sending a newbie on a competitive appointment is nothing short of a kamikaze mission.

Experience is one thing; aptitude is another. Which DISC profiles thrive in a role where a typical day consists of one to three listing appointments plus the steady stream of phone calls and emails about servicing existing listings? (Later in this chapter, we'll discuss building out your stable of transaction coordinators, who will execute 80% of the actual marketing and negotiation that bogs down the traditional listing agent.) Traditionally the DI personality type (high-dominant, high-influential) is the preferred player for listing work. The theory is that these personality types are the most persuasive and therefore the most likely to get the listing agreement in the bag on the first appointment. For the most part, I think that still holds true. However, I'm more open-minded after a few good experiences with agents whose DISC assessments are ID (and even one IS). Remember that DISC is just the leading indicator of someone's natural communication and behavioral style. It's been said, though, that intelligence is the rubber band that allows us to stretch beyond our natural dispositions.

Be sure that the direct, persuasive style that makes your listing agent stellar at appointment conversion doesn't come at the cost of the next, equally important characteristic of a great LA: empathy. Show me an agent who delivers great service to the customer, whose past clients are died-in-the-wool Raving Fans, and I'll show you a highly empathetic person who cares deeply about creating killer results for clients.

How to screw this up

It can feel so good to delegate those listing appointments that you may be tempted to hand them off to an agent and never look back. But one key mistake I made early on was not shadowing the listing agents on their appointments. When I finally decided to shadow one of my agents, I discovered that she was doing a great job building rapport but didn't fully understand how our marketing worked! Naturally, she was having trouble establishing credibility with the client and this was reflected in her conversions. We definitely lost a few listing commissions because her mistakes kept her from closing those deals.

Ideally, your LA is not an outside hire but instead an internal promotion from your buyers' team — someone who has consistently performed as a team player and brings energy to your operation. If you've done the heavy lifting of coaching and training (and pruning when appropriate) your buyer agent team, then you already know the quality of your best candidate's character and work. This makes good business sense for you and also demonstrates to your team that you are dedicated to growing each one's career.

Training your new LA shouldn't be a major project. Teaching the listing compliance package and the listing presentation and objection-handling should take about one week, including having the LA shadow you on three to five appointments. The following week, host a few presentations together, as a team. Finally, let the LA run the show and just shadow him or her, giving feedback after the meetings.

The new LA won't convert at your percentages initially, but give it a month to see if the numbers go up from week to week as the LA becomes more confident in handling common objections. Spot check occasionally by shadowing on appointments, but don't hover too closely.

Get More Juice out of Your Leads

Let's bounce to the buyer agent team for a second. It seems to be running smoothly, but how can you be sure that the agents are taking advantage of all the opportunities you've created?

One support role that can have an appreciable impact on the production of the buyer team is a Lead Coordinator (LC). The LC should carry the responsibilities of auditing your lead-management system for prospecting compliance from the buyer agents. Any missed opportunities associated with company leads should trigger a transfer of that lead to another, more responsible agent.

Your LC will provide value to you and your BATL by creating weekly reports on agent compliance with prospecting protocols. The secondary effect is that the sales agents will do a better job at lead handling if they know that someone is checking their work.

The LC will also spend a portion of the day calling leads to identify opportunities for the salespeople, and can go so far as to book those leads on appointments for the agents to handle. There are pros and cons to both approaches. On the one hand, having the LC nurture opportunities for the agents results in some great conversations between the prospects and the LC and time saved for the agents. But some of the same leads won't answer the phone when it's time for the salesperson to call. Likewise, if the LC books appointments for the agents, the prospects will often build too much rapport with the LC, which causes a bumpy handoff to the sales agents. ("But you're so nice, why can't I just work with you?")

The LC should be a part of the buyer team but also independent — willing to transfer under-contacted opportunities from one salesperson to another, without concern for any friendships with or preferences among the agents.

Compensation should be incentivized based on productivity. A modest salary plus a healthy bonus, based on a few percentage points of the buyer team's GCI on top of the baseline number of deals being produced at the time of adding an LC, is one idea. But any way that you decide to slice it, keep this in mind: As with any job that directly influences gross revenue, a personal investment in the success of the team is crucial.

The LC candidate should be an organized person who can also confidently talk to prospects for several hours each day. Your LC should get excited by prospecting and teeing up deals for the sales team but also religious about taking notes and scheduling follow-ups. On the DISC spectrum, an ID or IS personality with a moderate C is the ideal fit for this unique position.

Choose an LC who also enjoys teaching others. I'll show you in a few paragraphs how to get more juice out of this position by having this person double as a sales trainer.

Think Outside the Recruiting Box

One day you'll have the budget to employ a full-time, salaried recruiter. For now, you need to be more creative to minimize expenses.

Tactic #1: Create an agent referral program for your sales and operations teams. Everyone on your staff can be a part-time recruiter if they're happy (and incentivized). Your team members have plenty of friends in the industry. If they enjoy working for you and feel fairly compensated, they can provide powerful first-person testimonials about why it's great to be a part of the team. Great people want to work with other great people, so the candidates your team refers to you will usually be likeminded, responsible, A-player recruits. I think that you should heavily incentivize the recruitment of buyer agents.

Tactic #2: Hire a recruiter on a 1099 contract. Sound too good to be true? I thought so, too, until I saw our San Antonio expansion team lead use this tactic with instantly huge success. A hard-charging recruiter will find this opportunity very attractive. Consider paying out a spiff to the referring associate for each of the first four deals that their buyer agent referral closes. (This is preferable to a one-time upfront bonus, since it is inevitable that a buyer agent will sign up and then not produce any deals.)

Keeping a steady stream of new agents joining your team solves other problems downstream. When you need a listing agent, you look toward the buyer team for candidates. The same can be said for potential coordinator team members.

MARKETING & LEAD GENERATION

Right now, you should be reaping the rewards of the big lead-generation push that you made in the Awkward Teenager phase. You have brand recognition in your market and a sizeable listing inventory. Now you're playing in the big leagues, but how much more market share is really up for grabs? How do you grow from here, especially considering that the next logical marketing channels to explore are super-expensive and easy to screw up?

When applied to advertising, the law of diminishing returns tells us that at a certain point, more dollars spent on the same marketing channel will result in decreasing return on those additional dollars.

Radio is a great example. After you've established a foothold on four stations, you might find that stations five and six don't return much in the way of phone calls. You've already saturated the market, and throwing more money into the airwaves doesn't translate to more leads.

Let's go over some options for upping your lead-generation game and the highs and lows of each.

Billboards

A key advertising tool to consider in Explosive Growth is billboard advertising. Before I tell you how great they are, let me first get your expectations calibrated.

From a perspective of direct, trackable results, billboard campaigns have the lowest return on investment. Your ROI on billboards is an average of 2.5:1, which is very skinny. What's interesting about billboards is that you will start to see an increase in brand awareness among consumers when you roll out those boards. People will call in with stories like, "I've heard your ads for years on radio or TV and then today I saw your billboard. I just thought 'Man, God must be sending me a message that I need to call you to sell my home.'"

> There's a multiplier effect that comes into play when you add billboards.

What happens is that the billboards work with your other campaigns to create an echo chamber. There's a multiplier effect that comes into play when you add this layer of marketing.

If you were to measure the results of people who specifically say, "I'm calling because of your billboard ad," and don't mention any exposure to your other campaigns, your ROI would be in the dumps — maybe as low as 2:1. But the boards tend to boost your other campaigns and heighten your brand awareness in general. At this stage in the evolution of your advertising, you're going to have leads call in who say "I see you everywhere!" They can't point to the single source that made them want to call you. This can cause a lot of frustration when trying to track ROI. But again, these are champagne problems!

Just like radio, one place where billboards help to build brand equity is within your local community of real estate agents. This awareness can help you get talent in the door, and really high-quality talent to boot, since those agents are conscious of how expensive this echo chamber must be. They can see the writing on the wall that you are creating high-quality opportunities and aren't afraid to spend serious money in the pursuit of new business. They assume, correctly, that those opportunities will be shared with them if they join your team.

A natural time to add billboards is when you've capped out your potential exposure on the popular morning radio shows and TV blocks. There is a finite number of those opportunities, and once you've covered those bases, you've hit full saturation on the airwaves.

When it comes to messaging, the formula for billboard advertising is very simple. You will want to integrate both a brand equity plan and a call-to-action plan. What I mean is that there are different types of billboards you can buy. You can buy the big 14' × 48' billboards located on major highways. Those are going to be your most expensive boards. You can also buy what are called "posters." These are the billboards located on secondary roads and are much smaller.

What I recommend starting out with is a poster campaign to build brand equity and credibility. Keep the messaging short, preferably under seven words. For example, you could have a poster board with something like one of these:

- "#1 Agent per the Austin Business Journal."
- "Free Home Equity Analysis! Visit AustinHomeValues.com"
- "Thinking of Selling Your Home? Call Chris Watters!"
- "Need to Sell? Check out ChristopherWatters.com."

The seven-word cap does not include your name and phone number. Keep in mind that you may want to include a Fair Housing logo and any additional text required by your state real estate commission. Some states regulate real estate advertising more than others, so consult the rules carefully no matter what medium you are using.

You can add the big 14′ × 48′ billboards to communicate strong calls to action. With the extra space, you can afford another word or two. Here are some examples:

- "Your Home Sold, Guaranteed — Or I'll Buy It!"
- "Your Home Sold Fast — Or I'll Pay Your Mortgage!"
- "Your Home Sold, Guaranteed — Or I'll Sell It for Free!"

The key to advertising on billboards without breaking the bank is to subvert the traditional media buyers who charge a premium of 20 to 40% on top of the high rates that the mega-sized media conglomerates charge. Instead, find the mom-and-pop shops that own their own billboards. They are out there if you look hard enough, and they'll be priced at a significant discount, so you'll have more leverage in your ability to negotiate favorable terms. For example, a small outfit is much more likely to agree to a 6-month rather than a 12-month contract.

When thinking about costs, it really again depends on the market. In a city of two million people, a billboard on a busy secondary road is going to cost you between $350 and $500/month, while a board on a busy section of interstate highway could cost (at the low end) $3500/month and up from there. If we think about a board owned by a heavy-hitter media company and located in a prime placement area, we're talking $7000 to $8000/month. This price will be influenced by supply and demand. If you live in a city where it's hard to get permission to erect a new board, the supply is lower, which greatly impacts the pricing.

TV

In 2014, I had pretty well saturated the Austin radio airwaves and needed to find new ways to reach new prospects. Our media consultant pitched the idea of an endorsement deal with a TV real estate industry celebrity. We tried out for the endorsement and got accepted. Within weeks we were shooting commercials in Manhattan! It was a really fun time and the commercial spots actually worked. We received a good number of calls from high price point areas that are difficult to penetrate.

And just like that, we were on TV!

And just like that, we were on television! If radio worked for you in the Awkward Teenager phase, then chances are that television advertising will do well for you too. Investing in TV advertising requires that you follow a lot of the same tenets you applied to your radio advertising, with some important tweaks.

With TV, there are two different game plans. The first involves implementing a strategy where you voice the spot yourself and focus the whole spot on the consumer and what you can do for them. Instead of talking about how great you are, all the accolades and awards you've received, or how many homes you've sold, you need to sell the benefit to the consumer. What's in it for them?

The second strategy has a third party who is recognized and credible to star in the spot. Then, you get interjected in that spot, and the individual is talking about you and how great your company is (much like a radio host would) — personally endorsing you and lending credibility and excitement about the benefits that are in store for the consumer.

Let's talk about other variables to consider with TV advertising. The frequency and timing of TV spots are extremely important. With radio, you can have, for example, one spot play per hour between 7 a.m. and 8 a.m. and run it only three days a week — and you'll get great results. On TV, you need multiple spots per hour, and you have to make sure that they are played during peak times and, ideally, during shows that people are unlikely to record and watch later. Ideally, you'll run three times each hour.

The news block is the number-one place to run your TV ads. Start with the morning shows. In our market that's between 6 a.m. and 7a.m. for local news, then 7 a.m. to 8 a.m. for a mix of local and *Good Morning America*–type programming, and then again between 8 a.m. and 9 a.m. In the evening, we run during the block between 5 p.m. and 7 p.m. and again between 10 p.m. and 10:30 p.m. These are peak times when people are actually tuned in. Viewers generally don't DVR the news and therefore aren't fast-forwarding through commercials.

Spots for TV are typically 30 seconds, whereas our radio spots are 60. There are some exceptions, like special spots where you can sponsor the allergy forecast and have a little plug happen there. Again, it's about the repetition and serving as many brand impressions to the consumer as possible and in the shortest length of time. You really must perform an assessment of your market to make sure that you're advertising on the right stations at the right times of day — and that your competitors' ads aren't sucking up all the oxygen.

Whereas radio returns a 6:1 or 7:1 ROI, expect more like a 2.5:1 to 3.5:1 return on TV advertising over the course of six months. Obviously that will improve a bit over the course of a year as you build more brand impressions and more people hear about you.

Start with one station. As your campaign starts to produce results, you can test and expand to other stations. You want to advertise on the news stations that have the largest audiences, and you want to make sure you reach those people over and over again at the same time every day.

TV is very expensive. That's what negatively impacts your ROI. Depending on the market, cost can vary wildly. In small markets, you may be able to buy one of these 30-second spots for $50 to $100. In a larger market, you could spend $300 to $1200. But in a mega-market like Atlanta, Chicago, or any other city above three million in population, you could be looking at $1000 to $3000 for the same 30-second spot.

Tracking these leads is super-important, so make sure that you're directing TV web leads to a landing page that echoes the call to action in the TV spots. You also need to use a tracking number specifically reserved for TV leads.

Promotional Videos

Just like billboards, another credibility piece that you can produce is a series of professionally crafted promotional videos. Each video is a few minutes long and discusses a different part of your business. For example, you could create a video focused on your listing operation and another one that's about your buyer specialist team. You can discuss your unique selling propositions and feature interviews with your team so that it's not just you up there saying how great you are.

> Most of your happy past clients will jump at the chance to brag about you.

The other key is to fold in some client testimonials from real people. Think about your true Raving Fans — who would your ideal future clients find easily relatable? Most of your happy past clients will jump at the chance to brag about you.

For staff interviews and B-roll, think about attractive locations you have easy access to. When we shot our Austin team's promo videos, we were in the middle of moving offices; our old space was a mess, while the new one wasn't ready. As a fallback, we called one of the builders of a gorgeous new development and asked if we could use their model homes as backdrops for our interviews. They energetically agreed, and the videos turned out great. Check out a sample at vid1.wirbook.com.

Don't leave the opportunity to use video as a recruiting tool as well. Think about creating a clip that promotes your team to other agents. Have the interviewer ask questions about why your team is the greatest place to work in the industry. Make sure that you choose agents who are highly invested in your team and very likely to stay with you over the long term since you want these videos to hold up over time. (It's a mixed message for new recruits to see agents gushing about you on the video, only to find out when they come in for interviews that none of those people stuck around.)

The ideal place to feature the recruitment video is on a simple landing page for recruitment. Agent and staff prospects enter their names and email addresses after watching the video. The video really improves conversion and sets the stage for great conversations when you or your ISA gets the candidates on the phone. You can even promote the video on a special Facebook ad with a custom audience of real estate agents. How? Upload the database of email addresses and Facebook will match them with its user account database to render the video on specific agents' feeds. How cool is that?!

When thinking of where to place your buyer and seller videos, think about the most effective way to meet those prospects where they are, without being intrusive (i.e., no pop-over ads). You could send potential sellers a video prior to the listing appointment. Your buyer agents could also add their team's video to a drip campaign sent out to new website registrations. Upload the videos to YouTube and create easy links to insert into your agents' email signatures. Use your imagination.

There are some really slick operations out there that produce these kinds of videos, including a few that are specific to the real estate industry. You can check out more of our promotional videos at vids.wirbook.com.

Raving Fan Events

One of the challenges in building a team is the reality that the clients (especially buyers) are often more bonded to their particular agent than they are to your brand as a team. One of the way that can you can build stickiness between the company and the client is through throwing semi-annual or quarterly events that generate a lot of interest and are also affordable to produce.

Pie Night is a combination happy hour social and pie giveaway that takes place on the Tuesday before Thanksgiving. The whole team, including support staff, comes together a month beforehand for a call night to invite all of our past clients. (You also need to place reminder calls the week before. People forget.) Our team invites them to come by and get a free pie and socialize.

What we do is purchase 200 or so pies at a bulk rate from a local bakery and then box them up with a company logo on the top. The day of the event, we set up a bar with wine and beer for the parents, sodas for the kids, and a big buffet of nibbles. We also put on a Black Friday giveaway, where we display a few popular holiday items on the office TVs. We have the clients and their guests enter contact info for their friends who might want to buy or sell in the next year or so; we raffle off the holiday items to those who participate.

Here's a good invitation script that you can make your own:

Hey Sally! It's Chris Watters from Watters International Realty. How're you guys? I'm doing great, thanks — just getting ready for the holidays! That's actually why I'm calling. Random question for ya: are y'all going to be in town the Tuesday before Thanksgiving? Oh, you are? Good! Well, the reason I ask is that we're throwing a little event that evening. We'd love to connect with our friends, ya know, before everyone scatters for the holidays. We're going to be giving away pies from a local bakery, and we'll have food and an open bar. Oh and I almost forgot — we're also going to be holding a drawing to give away some Black Friday gifts, like a stand mixer and a big-screen TV for those folks who help make introductions to people they know who might want to buy or sell property around here at some point. I'm going to go ahead and reserve a pie for you; would y'all like pumpkin or pecan?

I want to point out two items about this script. The first is that you will never have an easier past client call than if you're calling and offering something valuable for free. No strings; let's hang out and reconnect, and grab a pie to take home to the family. The other thing is that you'll notice my language turning super-informal here. See, I live in Texas, and I know that by using the word *y'all* instead of *you and your family*, I can set a very relaxed and friendly tone for the conversation (the kind of tone you'd use if you actually want people to show up at your party). The same goes for *hey* instead of *hi*. You're off the clock and so are they; there's nothing to sell. Let that come through. Granted, *y'all* ~~may~~ will not work in New York, so think about what subtle cues you can use to relax the tone of the conversation.

Do we call the clients closed by agents who are no longer with the company? Absolutely. In fact, for our newer agents who need to build their sphere, Pie Night (and the preceding call night) creates a prime opportunity to create Raving Fans en masse.

How to screw this up

The cost of these events can add up. Watch your budget and, most importantly, make damned certain that your agents and staff are calling all of your past and current clients. I once threw a $6000 sports outing only to have 100 leftover, prepaid tickets because I didn't stay on top of my agents about confirming their guests.

TECHNOLOGY

Essentially we coasted through the technology portion of the Awkward Teenager phase. We made upgrades but didn't upend the basic way of operating that we established in Early Climb. Consider that the calm before the storm. The heaviest lifting you'll do in the Explosive Growth stage lies in creating one system that integrates all parts of your business to help you see the big picture easily and make good decisions.

Build a Custom CRM with Enterprise Functionality

The mountain of data that your organization has amassed since your Early Climb is staggering. Currently you're flying off of a stock CRM and a patchwork quilt of third-party applications that don't talk to each other.

First, let's list the things that your stock CRM does really well.

BASIC CUSTOMER RELATIONSHIP MANAGEMENT SYSTEM TASKS

- Manage lists of marketing and transactional tasks
- Record prospect contact information
- Create mailing labels

Let's think about some of the shortcomings of using a stock application and unintegrated services:

COMMON CRM SHORTCOMINGS

- Limited or no integration with your property search site to display listing views on the prospect's profile
- No ability to handle recruiting leads or manage HR for your hires
- No integration with payroll software to calculate agent commission splits and handle direct deposits

---

- Limited or no ability to store transaction documents

- No integration with the Google Apps environment

- Reporting functions are rudimentary; financial forecasting not available

- No access to the code required to add new features and integrations

- Transaction management is only a system of one-time reminders; no further accountability functions

- No ability for agents, team leaders and coordinators to work cooperatively and share information all in one place

For us, the solution was to build our own real estate business software on top of an enterprise-ready architecture. We chose to build our system with an incredibly powerful framework under the hood, which allows programmers to use code to help connect separate applications to one common database. Our objective was to create a system that is easy to deploy and ready for the real estate business.

For our system, we've added integrations with a ton of third-party systems.

OUR CRM INTEGRATIONS

- Accounting software

- Recruitment and hiring platform

- Payroll processing

- Property search site

- 15 lead sources (and counting)

- Custom HR database

- Automated email marketing for prospects and past clients

The system that we've created is a true enterprise resource planning (ERP) system, versus just a traditional CRM. If you're going to develop your

> *There is a tipping point on large projects where it just makes more sense to hire someone on staff than to outsource to contractors.*

own ERP system, be prepared to invest about 18 months in the weeds, doing heavy development and logistical planning with a software developer. Oh, and about $150,000 to get it up and running. That's about how much we spent in creating our system, and we're still spending to improve its capabilities.

So what are the lessons that we learned along the way? First, we learned that there is a tipping point on large projects where it just makes more sense to hire someone on staff than to outsource to contractors. We paid a huge sum of cash to a consulting group that never really understood what we wanted. The project manager left the team in the middle of the project, and no one else really took ownership of what they were creating. The whole experience was incredibly frustrating.

Customizing and deploying the software is time-intensive and requires that you work with someone, be it a contractor or employee, that you can trust. That party has to understand what you're trying to achieve very clearly and even help you articulate what it is that you want the system to do (since you are building processes that get very complicated, very quickly). The game changer for us was hiring a young computer engineer who had a bit of experience with the coding language we needed. Her hard work and creative thinking pushed us forward, and hiring her full-time with benefits was still more affordable than the hired guns. With contractors, the meter is always running.

The other tip that I would give is to devote a LOT of time up front to really thinking through everything that you want this system to do. Have all departments weigh in and create their wishlists individually. Then present them all together and see if there are areas where seemingly disparate functions intersect. Make a list of the third-party systems that you'd like to integrate with; do your research to see if those vendors have application program interface (API) interfaces that allow them to talk to the system. We found that some of the startup vendors we contacted were willing to do some of the programming for free. We created a win/win solution, since if they were able to build a bridge to the mother system, they could use that integration to help drive sales in the future.

It's OK to deploy in phases; you could push a version 1.0 that has basic transaction handling and buyer lead integrations; get that into the team's hands and collect a lot of valuable feedback before pushing forward with the other modules like HR and accounting.

I don't want to sugarcoat this at all. If you build your own system, the process will be extremely painful. The costs involved are staggering. I'll never forget the sticker shock of receiving invoice after invoice from developers charging in excess of $180/hour. But when the system is done, you can reap the rewards of integration and use your new machine to expand into new markets.

Perfecting Your Phone Game

Up to this point, your phone "system" is really just a patchwork quilt of agent cell phones, the occasional staffer's desk phone, and a recording and campaign-tracking program for inbound lead calls. (And it works just fine.)

Like almost every other system you deploy in the Early Climb days, you will eventually run to the edge of this system's capabilities.

PHONE PAIN POINTS

• Buyer agents become overwhelmed with "housekeeping" calls that are not sales inquiries. Other agents will call the number on your website that's intended for buyers to use, or the number on a yard sign. When your team is small, the annoyance factor is acceptable, but when you grow to 50 active listings, you begin to burn out your agents. Since you don't have a dedicated phone system, the agents are unable to transfer calls but instead have to look up the intended party's phone number each time, which frustrates both the caller and the agent.

• Important prospecting metrics like the number of dials, live answers, and total minutes spent prospecting are up to the agent to self-report. Self-reporting is problematic, especially when the agent knows that you don't have the ability to easily check the integrity (i.e., truthfulness) of their results. In plain English, expect that even good agents occasionally fudge their results.

- There is little or no useful integration between these basic phone system elements and your CRM. If Bettie Buyer is introduced to your company through a yard sign call and goes on to purchase a home and then refer four people to you, you don't have a mechanism to place her call recordings in her CRM record. You also wouldn't be able to alert the phone answerer instantly that this is a platinum-status Raving Fan who is calling.

To solve these challenges, I recommend combining two ingenious platforms: RingCentral (rc.wirbook.com) and TenFold (tf.wirbook.com). Let me explain a bit about the difference between the two services and how they work together.

RingCentral is a voice-over-internet-protocol (VOIP) phone system in the same class as Vonage and Fonality. RingCentral accounts can either be routed through traditional handset-type office phones or through a "softphone," which is a program that lives on your desktop or laptop computer. The system also sends and receives text messages and faxes, as well as provides an auto-receptionist functionality in case you want to create call menus in the future. As an administrator, you would even have the ability to listen to live calls in real time, and even coach the agent without the prospect hearing your voice. The system is a real game changer, plain and simple.

But the massive value-add starts with the fact that your team can also use the system through their existing cell phones. The RingCentral app on their phones allows buyer agents to prospect outbound and have their key performance statistics, including talk time and number of dials, uploaded to the cloud. Additionally, both in- and outbound calls can be recorded. (Check with the appropriate authorities for any applicable laws around recording calls.)

RingCentral has a robust API that is capable of trading information with powerful, top-notch CRM systems. That API allows it to also communicate with another killer app called TenFold. TenFold can create a popup window that allows you to access the CRM contact record for a prospect at a glance, as well as provide dialer functionality to eliminate time wasted on hand-dialing when outbound prospecting.

A fun secondary feature of TenFold is that it allows you to create a leaderboard for your agents and inside sales team. The leaderboard slices and dices the available call data to give out virtual awards for the highest number of dials, the longest average call times, and other metrics of success, which you can customize. In my experience, there are few more powerful motivators than healthy competition with the person in the seat next to you.

Improve Your Mobile Presence

In the Early Climb, we chose Proquest Technologies to provide the mobile voice routing (MVR) service to help in marketing our listings. Our experience is that the call volume produced by this system is strong, but there are currently some limitations that prevent the product from growing with a large buyer agent team of 10+ agents. The process for systematizing follow-up and many of the leads tend to get lost in the shuffle. Still, the system rocks for teams just starting out and not so completely inundated with leads that they're unable to follow up.

There is another system that you might consider, called VoicePad (vp. wirbook.com). The system is more expensive but very feature-rich, and it includes a GPS-enabled mobile website for each agent. The prospects can either call the number on a yard sign or they can text for more information. The system is constantly being improved and new features added, like social media automation and a flyer engine that automatically creates brochures for each listing.

Each listing has a personalized voice presentation that is played for the callers, and the system integrates automated SMS text messaging to send links to photos and the property search site. You can add partners (lenders, brand ambassadors, etc.) that can be assigned to the leads as well, where appropriate.

Each market is a little different, so you may have to experiment with different types of signs (e.g., secondary yard signs versus riders) and numbers (1-800 versus local) to see which of these variables delivers the highest number of calls. You may find that hiding the text option returns more results as well.

Sharpen Your Hiring

Once you've created some success stories by helping agents quickly grow their production, word gets out pretty fast. Organically, you'll begin to receive more leads from your existing recruitment ads, combined with unsolicited inquiries from agent candidates who have heard about your results via word of mouth. Layer on the new brand equity from successful mass-media marketing, and you've got a recipe for garnering your pick of the agents in your market.

The new influx of interest can feel a little overwhelming for you and your Executive Assistant (EA). At this stage you could automate part of the hiring process by adding a screening tool to help look for personality traits that suggest a successful match between a candidate and the open opportunity.

One solid option that's geared toward the real estate agent community is WizeHire (wh.wirbook.com). The system looks at a few facets of organizational psychology and individual behavior to create a score that indicates the quality of the match. Using an expanded DISC profile assessment, you'll get answers on the candidate's potential for success in several dimensions, such as engagement and talent.

WizeHire can also create easy initial interview guides, which come in handy in keeping even the most experienced interviewers on track and the process consistent. The system can also work with other platforms to match the assessment results with relevant records in your database.

BRAND AMBASSADOR PROGRAM

For your top-tier and longtime loyal partners, the most valuable item that you can offer is . . . you. Your time and your experience are more valuable than the emphasis on direct referrals was in the Early Climb. Your vendor partners hold you in high regard; otherwise they wouldn't have stuck with the BAP this long.

Consider spending a half-day once a year with each of your BAP members. You're going to do deep dives into their businesses. I recommend hosting these sessions at the vendors' headquarters so that you can actually see how their processes work. It's a good idea to have their key players attend as well.

For your top-tier and longtime loyal partners, the most valuable item that you can offer is . . . you.

Having the management team's insights on what works (and what doesn't) can be very illuminating.

Keep your eyes peeled for inefficiencies. Look for processes that could be automated, paper forms that should've been automated long ago. Ask tough questions about what the owner and the management team think are holding the business back. Remember that many small- and medium-sized businesses don't have direct communication and free-flowing feedback as part of their company cultures. Don't be surprised if your presence opens up a forum for the leadership to share some uncomfortable truths with the owner for the first time. Help them think through, as a group, where they're getting stuck.

You may find that you bring a particular value in reviewing the vendor partner's expenses. A fresh set of experienced eyes can almost always find a place where a redundant service can be cut or a more affordable solution uncovered.

Keep the tone overwhelmingly positive even if you see a lot of room for improvement. Affiliated business owners are bound to already be successful if they're part of this advanced BAP group. You're there to find the upside and facilitate change, not to make partners feel like their businesses are being run poorly.

COACHING AND TRAINING

The focus of your coaching and training efforts in Explosive Growth is really on preparing your key players for new levels of leadership. If you're going to transform yourself from a manager into a business owner, you'll have to install competent, confident leaders who have all bases of your organization covered.

Once they're in place, you don't want to turn those folks loose without a reasonably well-defined teaching outline and a trove of training content and collateral to match. Create a running start for your leadership team, although you should expect that over time they will flesh out your curriculum and make changes where appropriate.

Systematize Your Onboarding

When your recruitment machine is humming, your buyer agent team leader (BATL) should be teaching a class of roughly four agents each month. Let's pause there for a second. Are you wondering why four? Even in the most productive of environments, you're going to have agent turnover.

Actually, more often than not, it's your high-producing environment that drives them away. Think about this. Any agent who's had that aimless launch experience with a big-box broker, feeling directionless and underemployed, has seen firsthand the drought of leads and opportunities that characterizes those offices. So when one crosses the threshold of your office for an interview, the leads and opportunities seem like Real Estate Candyland.

So what's the problem? The problem is that many agents think they want leads but really doesn't want the responsibility of calling them 6 to 12 times over the course of a few weeks. Somewhere around call number 3, these agents remember how great it was to sit on the couch and watch TV while waiting on the occasional referral. They thought making $150k would be great, but all that hard work and stretching outside the comfort zone is a bridge too far.

To get to one good agent — a true keeper — you will hire two or three others who don't work out. It's just the way it is.

How does this relate to our topic? To scale and build a large buyer team, you will need to hold a new buyer agent class each month. If your BATL is ever going to get anything done, you need to provide some help in teaching those basic scripting and technology classes. Given the fact that the initial training is very heavily focused on lead conversion and phone prospecting, your lead coordinator (LC) is a natural choice to help the new agents find their footing.

Have the BATL and LC create a program for the first 30 days of training. Load it up with all those things that you forget to teach when a new agent comes onboard. Think about your core values, your story, your mission, and your culture. New agents have no idea what to ask when it comes to those items, so train your LC to take a couple of hours and talk just about who you are as an organization. From there, the 30-day training is easy to write; it's tech tools, scripts and objection handling, lots of role play and repetition.

An LC who is compensated based on the total production of the buyer team is well incentivized to help retain agents and make sure that they are productive and get there quickly.

Create Your Own University

Remember when your then-new buyer agent team lead (BATL) basically rode in on a white horse during the Awkward Teenager stage and saved your sanity by taking over agent training? Part of the BATL's job description at that time was to teach classes and to record the trainings. It's time to use all of that content to help you in streamlining your training experience.

First, take an inventory of the instructional videos and training collateral that you have already on hand. Work with your BATL to compare that inventory with a list of all the classes and one-off sessions held for each new cohort of buyer agent recruits. Your BATL will be able to tell you where there are gaps in the recorded material and create a list of new content that should be created to close those gaps. Assign that list to your BATL, with a reasonable amount of time to complete the content.

When your content is ready, you'll want to deploy online training software that is capable of hosting content and monitoring student progress. There are several good options out there, but our hands-down favorite is Kajabi (kajabi.wirbook.com). It's so simple and straightforward, and I love that the development team is continually pushing updates and improvements.

Kajabi allows for segregating your training into different products, so that you can create a curriculum for buyer agents, inside sales, or listing managers and keep them all separate. The system lets you combine your video lessons with any downloadable collateral like training guides, listing presentations or audio files. You can create text-only lessons or combine media to capture the attention of folks with different styles of learning. (I don't recommend getting bogged down in making each lesson a multimedia experience; get the first batches of training uploaded and then go back and make them slicker if you want.)

Kajabi allows you to upload your videos and compress them so that they stream easily even on mobile devices. It even integrates with the Stripe credit card processing service in case you someday want to charge for your training (or collect an upfront deposit that's refundable when the agent closes the third deal, etc.).

Providing the content for training is one thing; monitoring progress through a course is another. While Kajabi tracks students' journeys in the sense that it can tell you who has watched an entire video, we want actual confirmation that the lessons are sinking in. I recommend incorporating a testing service like ClassMarker. This tool is incredibly easy to use; simply create a quick quiz for each topic, consisting of five or so questions, and use the code provided by ClassMarker to embed a test into each lesson. You can set the system to email you and the BATL when a student has completed a test. Those notification emails also contain the percentage of questions answered correctly. Knowing that someone is keeping tabs on their progress tends to motivate the students to be more engaged with training.

An advanced use of your training platform could involve creating internal designations that agents and staff can achieve by completing prescribed series of lessons (and practical tasks, if you like). Think about the designations out there being sold to agents by agent associations and others. If you've taken a few of those classes, you know that much of the information is incredibly basic, general, and often very dated. I'm amazed by how much money is spent

Create a culture that celebrates constant improvement.

on worthless certifications. In the end, all you get is another acronym for your business card — one that is meaningless to the public.

Still, agents are people, and people want to feel like they're moving forward in their professional pursuits. So why not build levels of achievement in your own organization by creating specific, valuable, advanced-level content that actually pushes agents forward in their work? Every level should help agents develop skills that have material impact to production numbers, net promoter scores, or some other measureable item.

Make obtaining certain certifications a prerequisite to advancement within your organization. When one of your team members achieves a designation, make a big deal out of announcing the achievement to your team. Create a culture that celebrates constant improvement.

BACK OFFICE

Perhaps the greatest pain point of the Awkward Teenager phase is the extreme pressure put on you and your executive assistant (EA) to handle the spike in listings created by your new marketing. Mistakes happen, and the net promoter scores may suffer a dip while you are in the weeds with these deals.

In the Explosive Growth phase, we're going to remake your back office and provide solutions to systematize customer service in a way that creates a predictable, dependable rhythm to each transaction (and super-satisfied clients).

Build Your Coordinator Team — Part I

The model that we built is based on the knowledge that the results will be multiplied if all of our team members are in positions that play to their individual strengths. The same personalities who are effective persuaders

---

in the sales appointment are probably not the ideal choices to manage customer satisfaction and compliance. But that's exactly the prescription in the traditional real estate model: a jack-of-all-trades who is expected to perform every task from marketing to lead conversion, building websites to negotiating deals. It may sound like common sense, but great salespeople need to be out there doing what they do best: selling.

The listing transaction coordinator (LTC) is the backbone of our service-delivery machine. The LTC is the account manager, if you will; while the LA is out there as the face of the company on appointment after appointment, the LTC is back at the office making the sale happen. For simplicity, when explaining the LTC's role to the client, it may be helpful for the LA just to refer to the LTC as his or her assistant. People understand what an assistant does; but the general public does not know what an account manager does.

It's really important when you're talking to consumers that you don't get them confused about all of the different types of positions within your organization. We've tested this and even lost listings because we would send our salespeople on appointments to meet potential sellers and, when we tell them about our team concept and about every single player who will be touching their files, they get overwhelmed. They're fearful that they're not going to know who to talk to. For the last five or six decades, the traditional listing process is that you have a listing agent that's helping you sell your home, and they do everything (albeit with varying degrees of competence in each area). It's not ideal by any stretch of the imagination, but it's simple to understand.

It's important that the consumer understands that the listing agent is the one who is steering the ship. What happens behind the scenes is irrelevant in the eyes of most consumers as long they're seeing results.

Effectively, the LTC manages the listing manager (LM) and the virtual assistant (VA). The performance of these two employees and their execution of repetitive tasks is critical to delivering on the promises made in the listing appointment. The LTC delegates the work of coordinating photos, sign delivery, staging, etc., to the LM to get the listing ready during the "Coming Soon" stage. The VA can handle the tasks of managing the internet marketing and any special tasks like creating single-property websites for the

How to screw this up

The LTC role has to be a very specific personality. Being detail-oriented is important, but many extremely detail-oriented people have an internal narrative along the lines of "I'm smart and everyone else is stupid. . . . They should just do things my way." When a moderate amount of stress is applied to that personality, they lash out at clients, alienate cooperating agents, and create a negative vibe in the office. We've made that hire before, and found that most of these people are unable to overcome this particular personality defect.

listing or designing a newspaper advertisement when appropriate. The LTC communicates with the client about these tasks (because we want to limit the number of people contacting the seller), but they're executed by the two assistants.

The LTC is the main point of contact for the clients Monday through Friday, 9 a.m. to 5 p.m. Outside those hours, the clients know to call the LA's cell phone.

The LTC is usually an IS or SI personality, but with a strong dose of C. That personality type is a systems-oriented, highly conscientious personality who is a ninja at the details but also enjoys social interaction.

The ideal LTC has a lot of recent transactional experience. Some of the best LTC candidates are sales agents who enjoy the transactional elements and serving clients but find that they are unable or unwilling to constantly be generating leads and prospecting on the phone.

One of the best ways to find agents who have the transactional experience and are looking for the stability of salaried income is by utilizing email blasts to the agent community. Here's an example:

Subject: Hiring Real Estate Agent w/ Salary!

Body: Hey there! I'm a top-producing agent in town and I need help! I'm looking for someone who really enjoys real estate but doesn't like the sales aspect of it. If you're interested in talking more, please give me a call.

The typical day of a LTC involves getting new listings onboarded (with the help of the LM and VA) and serving sellers while they wait for offers to come in. When an LTC receives an offer on a property, it's the LTC's role to brief the LA and then to begin the negotiations.

Because of the intense focus achieved by the LTC working on a short list of service delivery tasks all day, every day, one LTC can handle 50 to 75 files in different statuses. Since pending files take up the most time, one LTC should work on a maximum number of 15 pendings on a consistent basis. (If you bump to 20 for one or two months, the load is still manageable, but if this pattern continues, it's time to look at hiring another LTC. Champagne problems, right?) With the rest of the files spread across less time-intensive actives and coming-soon listings, the workload is doable for a focused and competent person.

There are two key performance indicators (KPIs) that tell you that your transaction coordinators are doing a great job. First, the most important KPI is the net promoter score (NPS). Happy clients make for great online reviews, which helps deliver more leads and easier conversions.

So what are some of the key items that I've found contribute the most to a glowing NPS score?

Weekly success calls are crucial. All of our LA's come into the office on Wednesday mornings at scheduled times to call all actively marketed listings for weekly check-ins. You might think that the consumer's opinion is mostly developed based on your team's skills and service after the deal goes under contract, but we've found that the active stage is the make-or-break period for NPS scores in most situations. The reason is that anxious sellers feel forgotten easily, and when your LAs are juggling so many

> There is a natural tendency to skip over those sellers who aren't squeaky or whose listings don't have a lot of activity to discuss.

listings at once, there is a natural tendency to skip over those sellers who aren't squeaky or whose listings don't have a lot of activity to discuss. We used to list the property, work on the marketing, and not update the client until we had an offer. We created amazing results for people and still received NPS marks that were lower than expected. When we sourced the feedback, we found over and over that the complaint was the same — "I didn't hear from you guys enough." So the weekly call was born as a way to systematize that communication and for LAs and LTCs to hold each other accountable for reaching each client on a regular basis.

A side benefit of the weekly success calls is that the team approach that we promoted so heavily to the client during the listing appointment becomes apparent when you have both the LA and LTC on the phone with the seller. The LA and LTC have an opportunity to demonstrate each week how they really are two halves of the same brain when it comes to getting this person's listing sold. That demonstration builds trust with the clients and gives them more confidence when dealing with only the coordinator.

Let's take a second and expand on that idea of keeping sellers in the loop. There are also some semi-automated tools that can help you satisfy those sellers who are eagerly awaiting offers. Some online portals like Zillow/Trulia and Realtor.com have an option to email the sellers weekly statistics on how their listings are performing online. These reports can help your LAs and LTCs when it comes to suggesting price reductions; if our job is to get the home in front of as many eyeballs as possible, we can demonstrate that we're doing our part but we need the seller to price the home with the market.

> At the closing table, provide a form for the clients to fill in referral leads.

The second KPI for LTCs is the number of referral leads that they generate. On the initial listing presentation, the LA shows the sellers a slide titled "Our Promise," which lays out our plan for contacting them each week, for executing our exhaustive marketing checklist, fiercely negotiating on their behalf, etc. It goes on to set the stage for a referral ask at the end of the transaction. The slide says, "After we follow through on these deliverables and exceed your expectations, we're going to ask you at the end of the transaction to introduce us to people you know who may need to sell or purchase a home. Is that a deal?" Because the LA hits this note, clients have an expectation that we'll be coming around near the closing date to find out who they know that we should get to know as well.

The LTC should remind the happy clients the week before closing to be thinking of those folks to whom they can introduce us. At the closing table, provide a form for the clients to fill in those referral leads.

Build Your Coordinator Team — Part II

The transaction coordinator role on the listing side is invaluable; that person is the key to getting your salespeople back on the road and bringing in new business. But what about the buyer's team? How does a transaction coordinator work on that side of the business?

The buyer transaction coordinator (BTC) is hired at the point when your buyer team has produced over 15 transactions for three consecutive months. The BTC can easily handle 30 pending files at any given time. The buyer side transaction fee can underwrite the cost of hiring the BTC. A $495 transaction fee collected on 80% of buyer transactions can be a great way to zero-base the cost of this additional help. The pay is a competitive salary plus a per-file spiff.

The BTC can provide massive value to your buyer clients and their agents. The nature of the BTC's work is similar in some respects (think negotiation, transactional follow-through items) but very different in others. Because there is no property to get ready, pictures to take, or marketing plan to design, the BTC doesn't get involved with the client until there's an actual pending purchase contract.

Like the listing transaction coordinator, the BTC needs to be a licensed agent with transactional experience. The preferred personality type is SC. You may be wondering why there is no requirement for a higher I. The buyer agent representing the client has forged a much deeper connection and is quite far along in the process when the BTC is introduced. So the key thrusts are much more about perfecting the details of the consumer experience after contract execution, and keeping the deal running smoothly.

At the point when the buyer's purchase contract executes, the buyer agent will introduce the BTC to the client. The BTC's first function is to explain his or her role to the client, and then to get to work helping the buyer schedule inspections and connect with critical vendors like home warranty providers and insurance carriers. The BTC then checks in with the lender to make certain that the loan officer has a copy of the contract and is aware of the projected closing date.

The BTC also helps the buyers by taking over, in total, the responsibility of negotiating repairs after inspections. BTCs help clients schedule walk-throughs and vendor visits and performs regular check-ins with the buyer's lender to ask probing questions to make sure that the deal is still on track to close on time. Since the BTC's hours are Monday through Friday, 9 a.m. to 5 p.m., the buyer agents know to not let their inspection periods expire on weekends or holidays if they want the BTC to handle their repair amendments.

Our net promoter survey asks the clients to rate their satisfaction with BTC performance and asks for feedback on items for improvement, just like it does for the agents. Additionally, the BAs are surveyed periodically for anonymous grading of and feedback on the BTC.

Focus Your Assistant

In the Awkward Teenager stage, the executive assistant (EA) had a heck of a job description. In addition to the payroll and basic financial functions of the job, the EA was also expected to serve double duty as the TC before a full-time coordinator could be hired. Now that the TC role has been filled by someone else, your EA will be able to grow into a full-fledged office manager (OM). (Unless it turns out that your EA will make a killer TC. If that's the case, embrace it. You can find someone else to run the office.)

What are the duties of the OM? I call my OM my implementation ninja. For example, let's say that I wanted to launch a new initiative (could be marketing, tech, whatever). I'd need to research the field, source three vendors, collect bids, and use them to negotiate against one another — and finally, to greenlight the project and oversee its execution. In Explosive Growth, I have just enough bandwidth to get a project like this started off in

> *To reduce the chance that you're being gouged by a vendor, make sure that all the vendors list the specific listing address or other unique project identifier for each line item. Let them know up front that you don't pay invoices without this info.*

haphazard fashion and probably never pick it up again. The OM's discipline helps me take things from idea stage to reality.

The OM's next priority is to control the purse strings of the operation. He or she works with you and the accountant to set a monthly budget for your departments, and then makes sure that you stick to it. The OM is responsible for combing through all of your invoices from contractors to make sure that you're paying your bills without being overcharged. (To reduce the chance that you're being gouged by a vendor, make sure that all the vendors list the specific listing address or other unique project identifier for each line item. Let them know up front that you don't pay invoices without this info.) Additionally, the OM is perpetually reviewing credit card charges to look for redundant services or other expenses that can be eliminated. Paying as many of your bills as possible with a credit card can help the OM spot errors or inefficiencies at a glance.

The OM also makes sure that payroll is done and projects like end-of-year tax documents are issued. If you haven't adopted an enterprise resource planning (ERP) system, payroll can become a monumental task once you have 20 agents and 5 staffers. Transaction coordinators will have different salary and bonus packages based on experience level and whether they're serving buyer or seller clients; listing agent commission splits are radically different from those of the buyer agents. Often, various lead sources have different splits attached as well. Those agents who have been with you since the Early Climb days may be grandfathered into commission splits that reflected those early days when your team was light on company-generated leads to share. The variables and potential combinations are endless. The point: payroll can be a major project that occupies your OM for two to four working days each month if it's all being done by hand.

How to screw ~~this up~~

It's important that the OM balances out your weaknesses. If you hire someone too much like you, you'll screw this up.

At this stage of your business's development, the list of people who want a piece of your time seems to grow longer each day. Almost any personality type who starts a team will find themselves doing a certain amount of double-booking, forgetting appointments entirely, and overpromising in general. Your OM helps by keeping this syndrome in check (and doing damage control when it happens anyway). More than just helping you meet your short-term obligations, the OM can help redirect you when you see a shiny object and start to veer away from your strategic plan. To do this, your OM needs to know that it's safe to correct you; he or she has to have license to communicate concerns in a way that is direct and even confrontational when required.

Side note: I think that it's important for you to share an office with your OM. Close proximity benefits you both, as the OM can do a better job of managing you and your commitments if he or she can you hear when you put yourself on the hook to do something. I would also make sure that the OM has an open line of communication with your spouse, who can help keep the OM in the know on any personal commitments that would affect your availability to conduct business.

At this stage, the OM also coordinates the recruitment process by handling the online screening, booking the promising candidates on the appropriate team lead's calendar, then confirming appointments, etc. Your OM can sit in on enough interviews to learn what you're looking for in the applicants for each position and can also extend offer letters, sign up new agents and employees with their HR docs, and be the keeper of office keys, building entry cards, office computer passwords, and other miscellany.

> *Working with the same professional allows you to develop a signature style of listing photography and to be confident that you'll get the shots that you want, the way that you want them, each time.*

Bringing Photography and Courier Service In-House

Until now, you've been paying out roughly $100 for each listing's photos. Contract real estate photographers work with many different agents, and so the ability to take high-quality photos the way you want them is going to vary with the photographer's availability. Working with multiple contract photographers results in uneven results from listing to listing.

If you are taking 30 listings per month, it is much more practical to have a photographer on staff full time so that you don't have to worry about another agent's job taking priority over yours. Another benefit of using a staff photographer is that the quality of your photographs will become a hallmark of your service. Working with the same professional allows you to develop a signature style of listing photography and to be confident that you'll get the shots that you want, the way that you want them, each time.

You'll hit a certain point where your volume is too large for a contract-based courier service (which in the beginning could be the neighbor's 17-year-old kid and his pickup truck), and you'll want to bring someone on full time for the sake of cost-efficiency and dependability. The number of new listings that will necessitate this change is hard to pin down since the geographic size of your area and degree of added difficulty from traffic congestion will matter more than volume.

You could start by sourcing someone to work part time first, collecting 1.5X minimum wage or plus gas expense for hauling around flyers, signs, flyer boxes, lockboxes, and the like. You could look for existing single-operator courier services to see if they have the bandwidth (although Craigslist works great for this type of posting as well).

Add a Technology Officer

We alluded to bringing in a full-time technology person when we discussed building out your own real estate ERP system. There are additional other demands that will likely push you in the direction of bringing on full-time help with your tech "stuff."

The reality is that your network is probably pretty solid at this point unless you've recently moved offices or changed internet service providers. But the hardware situation is a different story. Your buyer agents are on their laptops, while staff are on various PCs that you've picked up along the way. These systems will have varying capabilities based on age, operating system, and most importantly, user competence. By this point in your team's growth, you've probably had about all of the Windows troubleshooting that you can stand.

> By this point in your team's growth, you've probably had about all of the Windows troubleshooting that you can stand.

Some of these headaches can be prevented by sticking to your guns when it comes to making sure that every person who works for you has been through a practical interview as detailed in the Early Climb chapter. Screening for technology-challenged employees and agents can stave off the need for a full-time technology hire for a while, but eventually you will need to fill this role. Even if you're not building out an ERP, you'll need support in areas like web design and editing, basic security functions, and hardware/software support. If you're not using an all-in-one ERP, then your tech specialist is going to have a dozen or more systems to manage (which includes manually moving information from one system to another and then reconciling all of that data).

If you are using one or more virtual assistants, you will probably also have to use a virtual PC setup that involves your VA logging into a computer in your office; otherwise, he or she will not be able to access internet marketing sites like Craigslist, etc. These setups are finicky and go down often. You'll also want a tech specialist around to help with web and data analytics to figure out what internet marketing campaigns are delivering results, or to run an A/B test on two versions of each landing page.

The technology specialist should be a generalist instead of a person who is expert in only one area of technology — and should be able to communicate well with both staff and vendors. (This sounds like a statement of the obvious, but remember that this position is partially about keeping the computer systems running but mostly about supporting and training the people who use them.)

Marketing Specialist

Once your average monthly marketing spend exceeds $20,000, you're going to need a full-time Marketing Specialist (MS) on your team to help manage campaigns and track results. The time that you personally spend on marketing should be focused on high-level, strategic thinking and securing partnerships (new media, endorsement deals, etc.).

> *Think of what you could do with an extra set of hands that are experienced in running effective campaigns.*

This full-time employee not only looks very closely at the sources of the deals when they close but also tracks the calls that come in for each campaign and how many of those calls turn into appointments. The MS will provide you with monthly reports on what kind of ROI you're seeing from each lead source and will use that data to make recommendations about where to spend more money (and what campaigns to drop completely).

The MS needs to have a thorough understanding of Google AdWords and all social media outlets, and some experience with radio or television is also a must. An MS should have experience in writing copy, as well as using marketing automation tools like Pardot or HubSpot.

Think of what you could do with an extra set of hands that are experienced in running effective campaigns. You could run targeted Facebook ads based on super-tight, one-mile radius areas that have photos of particular neighborhoods, asking users if they want to know what their home is worth, etc. You could send micro-batches of direct mail postcards for just-listed, just-sold and coming-soon properties. Or you could even have a unique Google Adwords campaign for each individual listing.

The reason that you don't need this person before you hit $20,000 in average monthly marketing spend is because prior to this time, you're relying on outside vendors for your marketing activities. For example, you could pay a contractor to administer Google AdWords for $500 to $1000/month, or a company like Vyral Marketing to facilitate your email database follow-up for roughly $500/month as well.

So you've made it through Explosive Growth. Are the burdens of being Captain Everything starting to fade from memory, as your staff and associates take on more of a role and, in fact, do more than you ever could alone? The satisfaction of seeing your organization mature is amazing. The only thing better is your Great Escape, which is what you've been working toward all along. The next chapter is going to show you how visualize your perfect worklife — and how to get there.

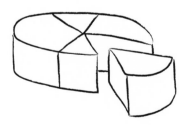

CHAPTER 5
The Great Escape

What does a Great Escape look like for you? After reading this book, is your answer the same as it was when you began?

Before we detail the key thrusts that are prerequisite for transitioning from management to ownership, you need to be exceptionally clear (and rigorously honest) about what you want life to look like on the other side. In fact, you must solidify this vision before you even begin the Early Climb. You need to begin with the end in mind.

> *You need to be exceptionally clear (and rigorously honest) about what you want life to look like.*

The only non-negotiable element of building your Great Escape is that all of this effort, all the sweat and sacrifice — the end result MUST give you the freedom to choose. Otherwise, what's it all for?

The freedom to choose is a state of mind. The Great Escape lies in creating a business that runs smoothly and creates profits whether or not you're at the wheel. The goal is to move you from Captain Everything to nonessential personnel. You can be entirely absent if you want. You can be engaged in the day-to-day or you can be the hood ornament of the company — not required to do much but sit there and look pretty.

I think that there's a clichéd image of absentee business owners who spend most of their lives on vacation, who pop into the office only to frighten underlings and sign a few checks. You won't get any judgment from me if that's more or less what you're shooting for as well (although hopefully without the frightening bits).

Your Great Escape may not involve vanishing from the office, never to be seen again. In fact, your Great Escape may not look like much of an escape at all to anyone but you. If you want to build your sales team to self-sufficiency but hang onto the operations department because it's genuinely fun to manage — fine, knock yourself out. (Side note: you are weird.) If giving up your listing consultations feels like losing a limb, then build your business to maturity and then cherry pick the appointments you want. Start coaching agents from other teams if that fulfills you, or hop a plane to the Sudan to make a difference in the world. Of course you can take that vacation, start the nonprofit, or open up an expansion office. Why the hell not?

---

*What does your vision for your
Great Escape look like?*

The kind of freedom that I'm talking about is not cerebral. I want you to experience that feeling of total independence to the degree that it becomes second nature. Here's what I mean. Have you ever experienced having a truly inspired idea — something that excites you all the way down to your core — and immediately something in your brain tells you that it can't be done? For me the thoughts were along the lines of "I can't leave / do that thing, I've got too much going on. My team needs me!"

The freedom I'm describing quashes that fear-based impulse before it can make its case. It comes from accomplishing what you set out to do. You own this team. You came by it the hard way, giving this business all of you, often at the expense of family time in the (relatively) short term. You fulfilled the monumental commitment you made way back at the first step of the Early Climb. Do anything you want now; you've earned it.

So what does your vision for your Great Escape look like? Can you see it clearly?

If so, keep reading to learn the final step that you must take to get there.

GET OUT OF THE WAY

Since I was a kid, I've always enjoyed reading interesting quotes from entrepreneurs and other people at the top of their industries. One of my favorites is a piece of career advice from Barbara Walters that was aimed at young people entering the workforce in their desired industry. Here it is:

Get your foot in the door. Do anything — if they want coffee, get the coffee — so what? Just be there before anyone else gets in, stay late, do your job, and then hope that you'll become indispensable. No one really is, but you hope so.

To be indispensable is to be secure in your position — in your place at the table. That feeling of security drives away the gremlins of scarcity and uncertainty. It also just plain feels good to be needed, doesn't it?

> "How can I let go if the team was built around me? In fact, at one point the team was ONLY me!"

Becoming indispensable can serve us so well when we're starting out in the business world. If fact, it's a great strategy for any long-term employee to adopt. But as entrepreneurs we have to shed that old, comfortable way of thinking. Weaving yourself into the fabric of your business to a degree that staff can literally not imagine the operation without you will create that exact result — a team that cannot operate without you.

You're probably thinking right now "How can I let go if the team was built around me? In fact, at one point the team was ONLY me!"

I want you to close your eyes and picture three buckets. Two buckets are large in size, and the third is small — tiny, even. The small bucket is yours; we'll get to the others in a minute. Remember the vision for your Great

Escape; where do you want to be involved in the business, if at all? For me, the answer is yes — I did want to stay involved in a couple of ways. I really enjoy the creativity required in crafting the marketing strategy each quarter. And I'm also really energized by helping to grow our company outside of the Austin area. So the marketing and expansion pieces go in my little bucket. Your bucket may be even smaller; if you just want to collect checks and delegate the rest, that's OK too. Add your favorite items to the bucket and close the lid.

Keep your eyes closed. Turn your attention to the remaining two big buckets. Let's fix labels to them; one bucket is labeled "Sales" and the other "Operations." Between these two buckets I want you to divide the rest of your responsibilities that aren't going to follow you into your Great Escape. Remember, your bucket is closed — the objective is to give away the remainder in its entirety.

Open your eyes. Draw a vertical line down the middle of a sheet of paper, and title one column "Director of Operations" and the other "Director of Sales." In its appropriate column, enter every function that's necessary to run your business. These entries should be broad; you can always get really granular later. Don't be surprised if you hit a mental block when trying to think of everything that you do. The list is quite long, and as managing brokers there are functions we perform automatically, from a "muscle memory" of sorts.

Go back through this book and think about the seven pillars of your business. Make sure that your list covers all of those areas and be conscious that some of these impact zones involve both the sales and ops departments in some way. Split out those subcategories and assign them to their appropriate owners.

Cruise through your last month or so of emails and calendar appointments. Calendar and email are the best representations of where your time actually goes, which may be different from how you believe it's being spent. Use the messages in your inbox to trigger any items you may be missing from your list. (And think of how awesome it will soon be not to have so many messages!)

All done? Consider this list your WHAT. The more important dimension, as always, is the WHO.

Look around. Who are the folks who've been with you for the bulk of this journey and have proven their alignment with your company's core values? Who do you know (or suspect) turned down more lucrative offers along the way, because they believed in what you're building? Whose instincts are the sharpest? Who would your team follow into a fire?

Are there two people who know your operation inside and out, command the respect of your team and whom you would trust to safeguard this amazing asset, your livelihood?

Your buyer agent team lead (BATL) is the most obvious choice for promotion into a director-level position. The breadth of experience gained in that role ranges from training sales agents to compliance and how to handle escalated client issues. It's likely that this person is the right choice for your Director of Sales role.

The sales director's primary objective is to protect and grow the company's top-line revenue.

To exit the day-to-day operations of your team, you have to know that the money is coming in. Think about the skills that your BATL already possesses and the areas requiring more training. It's likely that your BATL is very competent in the areas of sales training and holding people accountable to their goals. He or she has probably experienced success in fostering a healthy team culture, creating an environment where agents and staff want to stay.

On the other hand, the BATL may need training on the financial end of the business, including how to read P&L statements and the like. Some of the best sales team leaders fly by the seat of their pants; as long as they're busy and the deals are coming in, they feel successful. That's one of those tactics that works until it doesn't. Planning the sales for a quarter may be unexplored territory. You will need to make sure that your candidate is up to speed on your goals for the position, and that you've reviewed his or her plans on how to grow the team's production.

Because of the extreme cost of marketing, it's likely that you've made the decisions for all things marketing-related. If you want your sales director to take the reins here as well, expect to train for these competencies, showing the director or director-to-be how to negotiate with advertising outlets and track results once the campaigns are up and running. However, it is likely that your marketing specialist has a small team of outside vendors and becomes a director overseeing the marketing department.

If you promote your BATL to the sales director position, keep in mind that the BATL has been largely focused on buyer transactions and hasn't had as much exposure to the listing side of your operation.

The person handling the other bucket is your Director of Operations. While your sales director has a directive to capitalize on all available opportunities for revenue growth, your ops director is responsible for making it all work on the back end. That includes service delivery, client escalation issues, and, if you choose, the brand ambassador program.

On our team, the ops director also has one revenue-producing function that allows him to have a performance-based bonus in addition to his salary. Years ago I figured out that one of our largest revenue gaps involved the number of clients who sold a home in our market to move out of our area. Chances are that they're buying again in their new city, but since the listing agents weren't incentivized to highlight those opportunities for outbound referrals, they didn't do it. By the time we caught on to the fact that the clients were purchasing elsewhere, it was too late; another agent had hooked them. So since the nature of the ops director's role has him mostly dealing with the listing side of the business, we created a 10% incentive for each referral commission we get from an outside brokerage. Now the ops director checks in with listing agents to make sure that all clients are squared away and hooked up with trusted partner agents. This one change closed the gap in our process.

To be an excellent operations director, your candidate first has to be an excellent manager of time and people. This manager's first priority is executing on the promises made by the listing team; the second is to keep the machine running at peak efficiency. The ops director must have an intimate understanding of the workings of the organization — every computer system, every procedure in the manual. This person will become the guru, the end-of-the-line for compliance, contracts, and service quandaries.

The ops director is steady and unflappable. This role has more variety to it than the sales director role does since there is a broader array of functions that make up the operations side. I'm using "more variety" here as a euphemism for the reality of solving a couple dozen completely unrelated and seemingly random problems each day. Part of this director's job is to review the listing inventory and, where appropriate, recommend marketing adjustments or call the sellers to recommend price adjustments.

Our ideal ops leader came to us in the form of a buyer agent in 2012. While he succeeded at agency work, his passion was more for problem-solving and serving the client, as opposed to lead generation and telephone prospecting. When we entered our own Explosive Growth phase, we made him a transaction coordinator. He excelled in the role, garnering high marks from clients and coworkers. As we built out that unit, he organically emerged as a team leader for the coordinator group.

> *The sales director and ops director are two halves of the same brain.*

The sales director and ops director are two halves of the same brain. It is imperative that they work very closely together. Because their cooperation is so important, I suggest that you physically arrange your space so that those two have adjacent offices. Both of the directors must have a deep appreciation for what the other one does, as well as a genuinely friendly rapport between them. I'm not saying that they can never disagree, but professional respect alone is not elastic enough to keep such an interdependent working relationship healthy. In short, they've got to like each other or it's just not a match.

In total, the combined compensation for your director-level positions should eat up about 5% of your commission revenue. That includes salary and bonuses. It sounds like a lot, and it is; these are highly paid positions with enormous responsibilities. To retain true talent at the top of your organization, you're going to have to pay them well.

What we just did is install the capstone on your organization. Now your business is a fully independent, profitable asset in which you can involve yourself as much or as little as you desire.

Now that you can see the whole vision, are you ready to get started?

CONCLUSION

I remember what it felt like to start out on my own Early Climb. To say that starting my own team felt daunting is an understatement. The main reason I wrote this book is to lay out a roadmap for high-producing agents who want to expand their operations beyond what they could produce as sole operators.

When I started Watters International Realty, no such guide existed. I looked to famous real estate authors and thought leaders for books on launching a real estate career, and the options always fell into one of three categories:

- **The Unsubstantiated:** Largely theoretical, written by great motivators who had little or no experience in selling actual bricks and sticks. Great if you're interested in earning hypothetical commissions.

- **The Myopic:** Successful individual agents who teach the same stuck-in-the-80s methods for building a lone-wolf agent practice. If you loved Annette Bening's character in *American Beauty* and thought, "That's the career I want!", then this one's for you.

- **The Half-Baked:** These are books written for mass numbers of new agents and may contain some nuggets about building a team — but they don't show you the way to make it happen. After all, the authors aren't in the trenches and don't actually know how to build what they're selling.

Nothing out there felt innovative, and none taught me how to create a highly profitable team.

My purpose in this life is to help others succeed. I want to help push people forward in their careers, to help top producers build teams that actually invest in agents instead of "supporting" them (whatever the hell that means, anyway). When I started WIR, I wanted to build a proven, repeatable real estate model that creates extraordinary profits for our agents and partners through delivering immense value to the consumer. I accomplished that goal, and the next chapter in my story is to help others make the leap into extreme success.

I'M SENSING SOME OVERWHELM . . .

My hope is that after reading this book, some readers will become so excited by the prospect of starting their own teams that they find themselves jumping up and down on the sofa, Tom Cruise–style. I'm also totally aware that for every couch-hopper there will be someone who, right now, is feeling overwhelmed by the thought of stepping into risk, of leaving a brokerage that is comfortable but uninspiring. Such agents are aware that their current paths may lead to relative security but are certain never to lead to Explosive Growth, much less the freedom of the Great Escape.

If that describes you, it's OK. The enormity of the proposition I'm making in this book SHOULD spark a bit of hesitation and healthy fear. Like I said early on, no one would blame you if you read this book and decide that you'd rather play it safe and stay the course. You may need to invest some time in thinking about whether building a real estate team is for you.

If you know that you want more, keep reading. There are two ways to get started.

THE DIY APPROACH VS. GETTING HELP

For those of you who want to try to build a team with no guidance, my hat is off to you. I'm living proof that it can be done, but there were some incredibly painful (and profoundly expensive) lessons that I could have avoided if I had known then what I know now.

I can't tell you how badly I wish there would've been someone out there to mentor me on starting a team when I set out on my Early Climb. It literally pains me to think of the time that I invested into the wrong people, not to mention the untold amounts of money that I sank into the wrong marketing efforts and junk technology.

I wrote this long, detailed book to serve as a roadmap to building a team. For all the information in its pages and the hundreds of hours spent writing, it's still just a book. It's static; a snapshot of a moment in time. If you're old enough to remember navigating without turn-by-turn directions, you know that a map is a tool, while GPS is a solution. We use maps to the extent that they can help us. But they don't get updated when the city adds new streets, and they don't help us find an alternative way forward when too many people are crowding the same route. When we're lost, what we really need is someone to say, "You are going the wrong way. Turn around."

I've watched so many of my friends in the industry struggle for years with what I call the "greatest hits" of real estate agent problems: wildly unpredictable revenue, no work-life balance, and doing absolutely everything themselves. They operate from a place of perpetual financial uncertainty. That scarcity mindset makes them work harder (not smarter), as if their brute-force efforts are the only solution. They become strangers to their kids during the spring and summer sales seasons and overcompensate with expensive gifts at Christmas.

If you had told me in 2010 that in just a few years I would be helping agents across the country to build their own teams, I would've walked you into the psych ward myself. I've always had an entrepreneurial spirit, the drive to produce excellent results, and the desire for constant and never-ending improvement. But nowhere in my self-assessment did I see the aptitude for teaching others, nor the patience that being a great mentor requires.

Then, in 2014 I randomly had a conversation with my first cousin, Lori Horner, who at the time was an agent producing 25 deals a year in a mid-sized market in the Texas panhandle. She's also an amazing Super-Mom to four kids and has some big goals for setting them up with college funds and the like. We talked about some of her goals, and I half-jokingly suggested that she let me take her under my wing. We both realized that there was a natural opportunity there; since then I've guided her in building a team, as well as roll out advertising and technology strategies. She went from doing 25 transaction sides to 88 in her first full year — just shy of $300,000 in gross commission! I'm extremely proud of the growth that she's created through hard work and being willing to try new ways of doing things.

We also have a team in another major Texas city that's experiencing massive success by following in our footsteps. After seeing these guys experience the same kind of exhilarating growth as I experienced years ago, I knew that my model worked and that I had an obligation to share it with all agents who want more out of their real estate businesses.

I've been gratified to find out how personally fulfilling it is for me to help these agents lay the groundwork for building their own high-producing teams. Focusing on helping agents create businesses using the team-centric organizational model is incredibly inspiring, and watching those teams succeed has been an amazing reward for me. That's why I created the first real estate franchise system built around the team concept and engineered to help the right partners implement the strategies in this book. At the same time, we're continuing to test and experiment in our Texas teams, and we'll make those results available to our franchise partners in real time. Why? Because by "failing forward" with our established teams and documenting as we go, we create valuable intel for our franchise owners, who can't afford to try every new system or marketing outlet and who need visibility before they invest time and money in a new initiative.

With that said, I'm not here to sell you on using our franchise system. Brad and I live by a key rule: If it's not "Hell, yes!" it's a no. If you're not already excited by reading this book and the thought of working with us to scale your business quickly, then I can tell you right now that it's not a fit. Still, I strongly recommend that you find mentors in each of the Seven Pillars. Look for people who've actually created massive success in one or more of those areas. Line up behind them, do whatever it takes to join their inner circles, and soak up all the practical wisdom you can.

Whether you take this journey by yourself or fast-track your progress with expert guidance, I want you to hang onto this book. Underline in it and dog-ear it all you want, but don't lose it! This book is your guide for the next several years of your life as you grow a highly successful real estate team.

I hope you'll check out some of the free resources we offer on our website at bonus.wirbook.com and submit your questions about starting a new team (or fixing an old one). I'd love to hear from you about what challenges you're facing, what questions you have, and where you feel like you could use more guidance. Catch me at the contact info below!

And I want to THANK YOU for reading this book. The hundreds of hours of work that have gone into this book have been a labor of love, and I can't tell you how much I appreciate your interest. I mean it when I say that it's been an absolute pleasure to share my journey with you. I wish you all the success in the world, and I hope that you'll reach out and let us know how you're doing.

Sincerely,

Christopher Watters

chris@wattersinternational.com

512-956-7900

ACKNOWLEDGMENTS

I owe a great deal to so many people in my life. I give all the credit for my core values as a human being to my mom. She instilled in my brother and me the importance of perseverance, humility, and, most importantly, living life with a servant's heart. My aunt and uncle, Diane and Keith Watters, later gave me an amazing opportunity to learn the basic fundamentals of building a business during my freshman year of college. The skills I learned from them helped me later build a respectable lawn care and landscape business, which gave me the income to graduate from college without any debt. I have to thank the McGinley family, a former lawn care customer, for convincing me to get into real estate and taking me on as a buyer's agent. My next broker, Dial Boles, helped me understand the technical side of real estate and, most importantly, recognized my youth and devoted a great deal of time teaching me to pay close attention to the details. After forming WIR, I was blessed to meet Bradley Pounds, my business partner and the co-author of this book. He believed early on in the importance of building a team- and consumer-centric business. Brad is the most consistent and hardest working person I've had the pleasure of working with. He always goes above and beyond for his clients and the agents in our company, and he always has his eye on the bigger picture. It's also important I acknowledge all of the coaches and other industry leaders in the real estate industry who have helped us build an amazing organization. Last, I have to acknowledge my wife, Amanda Watters. I met her at a time when I was worth more dead than alive. She endured sleeping on a blow-up mattress and watching TV on a red Ikea couch held up by phone books, and she worked two jobs to support us. I'm far luckier than I could ever have dreamed. I've been given the opportunity to be connected to so many incredible people, who have made this journey possible.

— Christopher Watters

First and foremost, I'd like to thank Chris Watters for believing in me many years ago, and for dragging me kicking and screaming into team leadership. I also owe a great deal of appreciation to the agents and staff whom I've had the pleasure of training and mentoring since 2012. Their trust in us and eagerness to try new things allowed us to write a book that's not theoretical, but based in real-world experience. In particular, I'd like to thank Lori Horner and Chad Brady for their willingness to have their expansion teams serve as the laboratories that proved that our model is repeatable. Thanks to our editor, Kathryn Rogers of Rogers Editorial Services, for helping us communicate the message. Most importantly, I thank my husband, Shannon, for his patient wisdom and endless confidence in me that made this book possible.

— Bradley Pounds

You got
this.

Made in the USA
San Bernardino, CA
15 June 2019